Advance Praise for The Decision Switch

"Want to change the world? Start by learning how to make the best decisions that will take you to where you want to go. Jack P Flaherty's *The Decision Switch* can show you how."

— Shola Richards,
Keynote Speaker and author of *Go Together How the Concept of Ubuntu Will Change How You Work, and Lead*

"Decision-making is critical to our success and the influence of technology has made it more complicated than ever before. Too much information. Too many stimuli. Not enough time to think things through before opting to move forward or not. Jack P. Flaherty's new book, *The Decision Switch*, delivers a proven framework to consistently achieve the best outcomes possible."

— Sara Canaday,
Leadership Strategist, Speaker, and author of *YOU—According to Them: Uncovering the Blind Spots That Impact Your Reputation and Your Career*

"What would the world be like if we had a system to make better decisions? Jack P. Flaherty has created a system that can keep you on track and lead you to the best of outcomes. I highly recommend his new book, *The Decision Switch*. Keep a copy on your desk."

— Charles Todd,
Retired Principal, Deloitte

"Do you want to cut through the Gordian knot of a tough situation? Jack P. Flaherty is a word merchant who in his book, *The Decision Switch*, converts the pain of making tough decisions into the pleasure of achieving your goals…through his proven framework, which today's leaders can use when making critical decisions."

D0896171

"Jack has hit the mark again! Tackling an issue impacting virtually every industry and certainly within healthcare; a growing percentage of today's workforce struggle to make critical decisions confidently. *The Decision Switch* and the framework he's created, combined with an innate situational awareness and perspective on human behavior, enables Jack to connect with and drive sustainable results."

— Sheila Blackwell,
Healthcare Transformational Leader

"It's a simple equation with powerful implications for life and business: Better Decisions = Better Outcomes. In Jack P. Flaherty's new book, *The Decision Switch*, you will find a system for consistently choosing the right option and reaping all the benefits that making good decisions can bring."

— Bruce McEver,
Founder of Berkshire Capital and author of *Many Paths: A Poet's Journey Through Love, Death, and Wall Street*

"Jack P. Flaherty's new book, *The Decision Switch*, succinctly frames the risks leaders face when presented with a critical decision. The 7 Principles of Successful Decision-Making is a practical framework for making better decisions and illustrates the critical aspects every leader needs to consider."

— Mark Mooring,
President, Proper Authorities, and Retired Seargent and Co-Founder of the Los Angeles Police Department's K-9 Unit

"Jack P. Flaherty's *The Decision Switch* is a much-needed piece of work. His mission to help leaders make better choices and lead with confidence comes through loud and clear."

— Michael Parisi,
Head of Client Acquisition for Schellman

THE
DECISION
SWITCH

7 PRINCIPLES
OF SUCCESSFUL DECISION-MAKING

JACK P. FLAHERTY

CINCH &
STONE
PRESS

Los Angeles, California

THE DECISION SWITCH
7 Principles of Successful Decision-Making

 Published by:
Cinch & Stone Press, Los Angeles, California

CINCH &
STONE
PRESS

THE DECISION SWITCH is a trademark of Connacht Ventures, Inc.

Cover and Interior design: Kendra Cagle, 5 Lakes Design
Index: Russell Santana, E4 Editorial

Library of Congress Control Number: 2023907590

Publisher's Cataloging-in-Publication
(Provided by Cassidy Cataloguing Services, Inc.).

Names: Flaherty, Jack P., author.

Title: The decision switch : 7 principles of successful decision-making / Jack P. Flaherty.

Description: Los Angeles, California : Cinch & Stone Press, [2023] | Includes bibliographical references and index.

Identifiers: ISBN: 979-8-9881964-0-2 (paperback) | 979-8-9881964-3-3 (hardcover) | 979-8-9881964-1-9 (Kindle) | 979-8-9881964-2-6 (ePub) | 979-8-9881964-4-0 (audiobook) | LCCN: 2023907590

Subjects: LCSH: Decision making. | Leadership. | Management. | Success. | Goal (Psychology) | Self-consciousness (Awareness) | BISAC: BUSINESS & ECONOMICS / Decision-Making & Problem Solving. | BUSINESS & ECONOMICS / Leadership. | BUSINESS & ECONOMICS / Management.

Classification: LCC: HD30.23 .F53 2023 | DDC: 658.403--dc23

To my wife Shannon and my daughters Makenna and Sienna. Unquestionably the three best decisions I have ever made, and this one is for you. I will love you always and forever.

Life is simple.

Make good decisions
and good things happen.

Make bad decisions
and bad things happen.

—DICK VITALE

TABLE OF CONTENTS

PREFACE

Decision-making is one of the most integral functions of both our professional and personal lives. However, it is a skill set that has historically received little attention, and that trend continues today. Many of today's leaders, young and old, lack the training, mentorship, and tenure to develop the strong decision-making skills necessary to achieve consistently positive outcomes that enable personal success. In many ways, today's employees are rewarded for making safe and conservative choices, and not for supporting their personal ambitions or an organization's ethical, strategic, and growth objectives. I see our next generation of leaders at risk of not achieving what's truly possible, as a result of having an inadequate personal compass or approach to help them navigate the difficult decisions we often face on a daily basis.

A challenge I understand all too well. Reflecting upon the trials and tribulations I have encountered throughout my career, it is the culmination of personal experience, influential mentors, and observing my clients and their executive teams that I found there are seven critical principles that empower leaders to make better decisions. Principles that, when adopted individually or as a comprehensive framework, are woven into your personal decision-making process, will instill greater confidence in your conclusions, encourage more trusting and collaborative relationships, and, thereby, produce consistently more productive and successful outcomes.

The 7 Principles of Successful Decision-Making:

1. Triage First
2. Follow Your North Star
3. Collaborate with Others
4. Recognize Cognitive Bias
5. Establish a Champion
6. Manage Fallout
7. Practice Self-Reflection

In this book, I will share with you the fundamental concepts for each of the framework's principles, cultivated over the course of my career that served to help myself and others in making better decisions that resulted in better outcomes. Framed within each section of this book, you will find understandable descriptions for each principle, practical examples of tools I have adopted, as well as personal anecdotes and stories of real-world applications to elucidate why these are critical to your professional and personal success. As part of your adoption of the framework, the principles presented are not meant to be followed strictly in chronological order but rather based on the priorities and influences you encounter while you process and make critical decisions.

I wish nothing but success for you in your personal and professional journey!

Yours Truly,

Jack P. Flaherty

INTRODUCTION

Why **Effective Decision-Making Matters** and Creates **Consistently Positive Outcomes**

"You cannot make progress without making decisions."
—JIM ROHN

I have always been fascinated by the human psyche, particularly how and why an individual makes a decision. Decision-making should be a trusted and reliable core capability of every individual and organization. However, over the course of my twenty-plus-year career consulting in risk management, I have had the opportunity to observe thousands of my clients' decisions, many of which resulted in an unsatisfactory outcome, and, in extreme scenarios, the downfall of a company. The one consistent thread I found within each failure was the absence of a decision-making framework or process to guide an individual in making their conclusion.

While many see decision-making as an event, it is actually a process—a process that evolves over time. In fact, it's rare today for many executive leaders, both new and well-tenured, to have a go-to decision-making process. By not instilling a process, individuals frequently struggle to consistently make objective, timely, and effective decisions. Each of these aspects is able to invoke thoughts of self-doubt and self-destructive questions, and has the potential to cripple leaders due to an overwhelming sense of anxiety and uncertainty about the adequacy of their preparation and execution. Mind you, the effects of decision-making are challenges virtually all of us have or will face at some point in our careers. They are often instigated or compounded by internal pressures, such as an organization's culture and politics, external drivers, such as changes in economic conditions and regulatory policies, or the ever-present expectations of investors.

An example of this was Countrywide Financial Corporation. Once a darling investment of the equity community, their stock price rose a mind-boggling 23,000 percent between 1982 and 2003. However, this Cinderella story did not end in the fashion typical of a Disney fairy tale, as their fall from grace is legendary.

Evidence of the influence these pressures can have on a leader's decisions can be found at all levels of the organization. Starting with the culture and tone set by Countrywide's Chief Executive Officer (CEO) Angelo Mozilo, who publicly acknowledged establishing "aggressive targets"[1] for the organization to fuel its growth and thereby its stock price. Directives, along with the Federal Reserve's relaxation of lending standards, enabled loan officers and organizational policy-makers to design innovative mortgage product offerings that reduced applicants' eligibility requirements. These decisions increased the risk exposure associated with the mortgage-backed securities Countrywide packaged and sold to an insatiable customer base.

Now imagine yourself as a loan originator for Countrywide in the mid-2000s, a role responsible for evaluating an applicant's creditworthiness as a means of mitigating the risk undertaken by the issuer. And, yet, you were also responsible for carrying out the adoption of new programs and directives meant to drive production growth by targeting applicants who were essentially unqualified to meet their loan obligations. A precarious position, which in retrospect appears to have often overlooked common sense. It was these decisions, combined with the collapse of US home values in 2007, that led to Countrywide's quick demise and an ultimate fire sale to Bank of America in January of 2008 to avoid bankruptcy.

Today's technology-fueled and demanding business climate requires professionals like yourself to make on average 35,000 decisions a day, ranging from menial choices about what to wear for an upcoming Zoom call to life-altering choices impacting health, wealth, or potentially affecting the standard of living for millions of lives. Still, many of us fail to have a decision-making process that considers the complexity, magnitude, and impact of our decisions. Whether it's a lack of training, education, or mentoring, these can all lead to decision fatigue—the sensation of becoming overwhelmed by the volume of decisions we are required to make on a daily basis.

As but one example of the many types of decisions we're required to make on a daily basis, researchers at Cornell University estimate that 221 relate to food alone.[2] For anyone with children, this is a statistic you are likely to vehemently challenge. You are not alone, as I am right there with you. One of my daughters' favorite restaurants is the Cheesecake Factory, as they love the adventure of sifting through, inquiring, and contemplating their voluminous menu consisting of a whopping 250 different items! It's for this reason that, when short on time, I default to In-and-Out Burger and the simplicity of its menu—essentially composed of three items: burgers, fries, and beverages. Despite often having long ordering queues, their lines move quickly as there just aren't enough options to contemplate and, therefore, it takes someone less than a minute to make a decision.

Contributing to the proliferation of bad decisions is the impact, both short- and long-term, of our increased use of real-time communication platforms, such as texting, Telegram, and Discord. In addition, social media plays a huge part in our decision-making through posting or responding on platforms such as Twitter, Instagram, and Facebook. Each of these platforms was built on the premise of cultivating a continuous dialogue between participating parties. In many cases, I find there is an implied expectation to continuously monitor these electronic conversations to stay abreast and, therefore, leave little time for our actual jobs. I consider myself to be technologically savvy; however, when faced with a litany of priorities competing for my attention, I regularly fall behind on any given chat dialogue. When asked to weigh in on a question, I am required to spend an inordinate amount of time scanning through hundreds of lines of unstructured text and consequently scrambling to find the right answer in a timely manner.

In addition, our verbal and electronic dialogues are frequently littered with acronyms, abbreviations, and incomplete sentences, which means that you often need to "read between the lines" to fully understand the context of a conversation and what is truly going on. In the process of absorbing information shorthand, I found decisions become increasingly erratic and misaligned with the goals we are seeking to achieve. What's worse, and quite frankly disrespectful, is the active use of these services during in-person meetings, video conference calls, or even in the midst of a casual conversation. It brings into question, *how many of us are actually paying attention?*

All of this reduces our ability to enforce personal accountability because, God forbid, you're able to track down a written record stating what decisions were made, who approved them, and most importantly why. The informality in communications makes it increasingly difficult to gain a sense of our roles and responsibilities, as well as hold others responsible for their communications and actions.

As it turns out, outcomes are not based solely on the quality of a decision, but on the adequacy of the process and tools used to make the decision itself. The bad news? At present, there is an overwhelming absence of education within our schools and corporate development programs that has created a recognizable gap in knowledge on how to make an effective decision. Historically, this knowledge gap has been bridged through personal mentoring and on-the-job experience; however, the effectiveness of these methods is beginning to wane as well. The speed at which individuals are changing jobs and companies has made it more difficult to establish and maintain these types of relationships. In addition, the recent shift to a remote workforce and not having to go into the same office every day, has greatly reduced our ability to genuinely connect and learn from our predecessors.

The good news? There are proven tools and techniques available to assist with improving your decision-making skill set. Based on my experiences, I compiled these fundamental concepts within the *7 Principles of Successful Decision-Making* that I am excited to be able to share with you. You, too, can learn how to master the art of decision-making, and it's my sincere promise that it will positively impact the success and satisfaction of your professional and personal lives.

Why Good Decisions Matter

Mike Rollings from Gartner, a leading research and consulting firm, captured it perfectly on why decision-making matters: "The absence of an effective and efficient decision-making process has the potential to lead an individual or organization adrift, or leave them blind to changes in market conditions, customer perceptions, and behaviors."[3] Rollings should know, being the chief of research at Gartner, who publishes the lauded Magic Quadrant™. This is a series of market research reports that provide visual snapshots, in-depth analyses, and actionable guidance that is widely regarded and utilized by chief information security officers (CISO), chief data and analytics officers (CDAO), and software engineering leaders to make critical technology decisions.

It is effective decision-making, engineered to be connected, contextual, and continuous, that alleviates uncertainty and improves our ability to establish clarity and confidence in what were once opaque considerations. Possessing strength in this competency has the ability to become a key differentiator for you, your department, and even your company. Embracing these principles and educating your team on how to comfortably handle uncertainty with skill will establish a legacy for yourself and instill a lasting competitive advantage for your organization.

Prominence and Legacy

Leaders like yourself demonstrate their prowess and intelligence in many ways, such as cultivating a strong culture, setting the tone for their teams, and motivating their workforce. However, above any other standard, your perceived success and legacy will be determined by the quality of your decisions. Having led countless postmortem reviews, I have witnessed, firsthand, strong and effective executive leaders lose their positions over a single poor decision. Outcomes that were the result of a short-sighted decision that was made in haste or isolation. Frequently, we found that these leaders had failed to assess all of the information and options available before making their final determination. Indeed, my experience has shown that simply put, leaders often approach decision-making in ways that put their roles in jeopardy and introduce unnecessary risk to their organizations.

Look no further than the 2019 firing of Boeing's CEO, Dennis Muilenburg. Muilenburg had spent thirty years successfully rising up the ranks at Boeing and was eventually named its CEO in 2015. Under his leadership, the 737 MAX was to be Boeing's crowning achievement, an enhanced version of its predecessor with admirable objectives of significantly improving the aircraft's fuel efficiency and reducing its carbon emissions. However, Boeing's ambitions to satisfy their customers' demand for the 737 MAX created a scenario that led to a number of decisions that deviated from their corporate mission, which was "to connect, protect, explore, and inspire the world through aerospace innovation."[4]

The key word here: *protect.*

Despite repeated concerns raised by employees and the aircraft's test pilots about the design, safety, and training requirements, Boeing proceeded forward with the commercial launch of the 737 MAX and deceptively pressured the Federal Aviation Administration (FAA) to certify its airworthiness. As evidence of this, employee emails released by the US Congress during its investigation called into question the design and safety of the aircraft and even undermined the credibility of its test pilots to justify their assertion that the aircraft was ready for delivery.

As a result of my research of Boeing's handling of the 737 MAX program, under Muilenburg's leadership, they had made three key categorical decisions[5] that led to the fatal crash of three 737 MAX aircraft and ultimately the firing of Dennis Muilenburg.

1. **Ignoring stakeholder feedback:** Muilenburg testified before Congress, saying that "the company believed the plane was safe with additional pilot training, and … it was premature to ground the plane until more facts about the crash were available," despite repeated concerns raised by key stakeholders who concluded otherwise.

2. **Committing to false promises:** "After the second of the two crashes, Boeing promised that it would have a solution 'in the coming weeks.' But that proved … wildly optimistic, and the company missed one set of … deadlines after another in its attempt to win approval from the FAA to get the plane back in service."

3. **Failing to find a resolution:** Boeing's announcement that it would "temporarily halt production of the 737 MAX indefinitely," confirmed its inability to effectively identify and cure the airplane's design issues.

Looking back at each of Muilenburg and his executive team's decisions, one can easily conclude that Boeing's leaders viewed their decisions through a lens that did not take into consideration the safety of its passengers. Nor did they choose to consider alternative options, opinions, or solutions for the problems they had identified. Siloed decision-making and ignoring feedback from your employees and stakeholders impair your ability to make optimal and well-informed decisions, thereby eroding trust with your staff and stakeholders.

Siloed decision-making lacks the requisite collaboration necessary between individuals and departments. This will eventually lead to miscommunication, misalignment, and, in time, the downfall of an organization. Rigid decision-making goes hand in hand with a lack of transparency, which results in confusion and erodes stakeholder trust, as well as their belief in the company's vision and ability to achieve future success.

Event versus Process

Leaders who treat decision-making as an event view these situations as discrete choices taking place at a single isolated point in time, whether that's approving a purchase order, negotiating terms of a contract, or maybe even deciding to lay off one of their employees. This classic and antiquated view of decision-making is analogous to pulling your head out of the proverbial sand, observing what is in front of you, and making a decision based on a gut feeling, personal belief, previous experience, or all three. Such decision-making leaders move on without regard or concern for the results of their decisions or the impact they might have had on the organization, department, or specific individuals.

In a simplified example of this, a sales and marketing executive is faced with a critical decision pertaining to a previously successful product that recently experienced a significant decline in sales and whether to pull it off the market. An "event" leader would mull in solitude, potentially review current and previous sales reports, reflect on similar product campaigns, and then finally conclude to pull the product off the market. But to look at decision-making in this manner has the potential to overlook larger social, environmental, and organizational contexts that, in many cases, determine the success of our decisions. In this situation, a multitude of issues could have impacted the product's sales decline, including a problematic supply chain or onboarding of an inexperienced sales representative, neither of which relate to a lack of consumer interest.

Decision-making is a process, replete with organizational politics and discord at all levels of an organization. It is often comprised of numerous phases that include: defining your objective and requirements; procuring and analyzing the information available; assessing the potential impediments and challenges; and navigating the organizational politics and power plays that often influence our ability to achieve a desired goal. Research shows a striking difference between leaders who make good decisions that consistently achieve positive and productive outcomes versus those who make poor decisions resulting in frequently negative outcomes: a lack of knowledge about how to make an effective decision. In many cases, this is due to a leader's myopic understanding of the effort required to persevere in the face of adversity and an overconfident view of themselves, in that they alone control the outcome of a decision. The framework I have created for you is a deliberate and systematic approach designed to provide the knowledge and confidence required to make better decisions that consistently result in positive results and better outcomes.

Snapshot of Today's Business World

Having spent more than twenty years consulting clients on matters related to risk management, technology, finance, and business operations, I have had the opportunity to closely observe hundreds of highly effective leaders and decision-makers. I have also borne witness to numerous "failed" decisions—made by good leaders who simply did not have the requisite skill set to effectively make a quality decision—where most often the failure was due to an avoidable error.

Recognizing the absence of decision-making within the curriculum of our current education system, leaders have historically filled this void through coaching obtained from personal mentors. A once affable and effective approach to cultivating decisive leaders, I have observed a sharp decline in our access to effective mentors. A stark reality of the impact an increasingly transient and remote workforce has had on our ability to establish and maintain these types of meaningful relationships, as well as the adoption of communication and collaboration technologies, often eliminates the one-on-one coaching we once received. Look no further than the U.S. Bureau of Labor Statistics, which concluded that the average worker today will have held twelve different jobs over the course of their career.[6] A number that has the potential to increase, as Gallup reported in 2021 that "48% of America's working population is actively job searching or watching for opportunities."[7] As a result of the fluid nature of today's workforce, employees will not receive the same amount of mentoring as they might have historically.

Ultimately, this leaves our next generation of leaders in the precarious position of learning on the job. In retrospect, supervisors would often patiently provide an individual with the time and space to learn through trial and error, which has now been replaced with impatience stemming from today's results-driven style of management, due to the increasing speed of business and corporate pressures to meet quarterly, monthly, or even daily quotas. A scenario that leaves little opportunity for employees to learn from their mistakes.

The significance of decision-making, combined with a shortfall in education and mentoring opportunities, as well as the impatience of managers who expect employees to understand how to navigate the organization's processes and politics, often breed "cancerous" cultures of mistrust, finger-pointing, and complacency—each a deadly weapon that can kill an initiative, project, or company. Based on the knowledge I have gained, as well as having an ingrained passion for education, it is my personal goal to empower today's workforce with the knowledge and tools required to become decisive leaders able to make effective decisions at the speed their role requires and, consequently, achieve increasingly positive outcomes.

Personal Aside

I am not one to throw stones and not acknowledge my own failures. I, too, have struggled with and have made my fair share of poor decisions. At the young age of 24, I landed a highly sought-after derivatives associate position at Morgan Stanley. At the time their derivatives trading desk was the largest and most prestigious in the world, having well-regarded books written about its escapades (namely, *Fiasco: The Inside Story of a Wall Street Trader* by Frank Partnoy). I was a contract administrator, responsible for documenting complex trade details within contractual agreements. In other words, I memorialized the terms of trades agreed to within the now defunct "open outcry" trading pits of the Chicago Board of Trade.

In this role, I worked closely with a brilliant group of traders, salespeople, and risk management experts, all of whom came from the most prestigious universities throughout Europe and the United

States. The culture and atmosphere created by the diverse and highly educated backgrounds of my colleagues were infectious and drew me in immediately. It was my dream job and one where I enjoyed the quintessential investment banking and trading floor experience. Our trading desk sat on the fourth floor of our global headquarters, located at the corner of Times Square in New York City. The trading floor spanned the entire width of the building, larger than two football fields, and was filled with hundreds of trading screens and personnel. Frequently, we were the benefactors of lavish lunches delivered by renowned restaurants such as Smith & Wollensky and paid for by our brokerage firms. As a lifelong Yankees fan, I was often offered tickets to playoff and World Series games, as well as frequented some of New York City's trendiest clubs and bars. Having grown up in a small town in upstate New York with parents who both came from virtually nothing, I was blown away.

Twelve months into my position I had established one goal for myself, which was to get promoted to the trading desk as a trading assistant or "TA." These fortunate individuals were the right hand to traders whose annual income ranged anywhere from $5 million to $15 million a year. At the time, it was said that the head of our trading desk controlled 15 percent of the Eurodollar futures market, which in perspective, the global market value of interest rate swaps in 1998 was estimated at almost $1.5 trillion.[8]

Impatient with the pace of my career progression, I persistently inquired of the TAs whom I closely worked with about opportunities for promotion and would consistently receive the same answer, "No one has ever moved from your role into a TA position." In so many words, I was not even on the list for consideration. As a result, I eventually decided to quit and move to Los Angeles with my future wife. Finally, having gathered the courage, I delivered the news to my director and provided him with a letter of resignation. While there were some deliberations and sincere requests for me to stay, in the world of trading once you notify management of your intentions to leave the firm, you are done. There would be no turning back.

The kicker? I found out weeks later that I was to be promoted in the same week I had submitted my resignation. In this instance, had I sought out the advice and input of the true decision-makers, I might have been able to make a more well-informed decision. Since I initiated the termination, they'd assumed I was not up for the role and quickly found another willing applicant. I had lost the opportunity, not because I lacked the requisite intelligence, skills, or personal relationships, but because I had been impatient. I had viewed this decision as an event and not a process. I made the decision solely on my own, based on raw emotion and short-sighted views, rather than taking into consideration the decision-making knowledge and tools available to me.

The following pages outline what I have defined as the *7 Principles of Successful Decision-Making.* Over the last 20-plus years, I've observed that we frequently allow our emotions to guide how we approach our decisions, rather than through an informed and objective process. Every important decision you make has the potential to impact numerous stakeholders, and not just yourself. Recognize that our decisions are influenced by emotion and instinct, particularly fear and self-preservation. Each is a hardwired human survival response, often causing us to make knee-jerk choices based on self-doubt and how we will be perceived as a result of our actions. Conversely, when these counterproductive responses are kept in check and we allow ourselves to focus on an objective, we are far more likely to make decisions that bring us closer to the outcome we seek to achieve. It is my goal to teach others how to navigate this fear and master the skills required to make effective decisions that result in consistently positive outcomes. Adopting decision-making as a core personal skill will invoke newfound confidence in the choices you make, freeing up the clouded mind space anxiety causes, thereby allowing you to remain focused on the objective at hand and increasing your capacity to actively engage and lead others.

We all strive for success, and generally speaking, I feel most leaders seek the best choices available to them and that will produce positive outcomes as a result. The problem is that the world doesn't always comply with our wishes. Following what we believe to have been a good decision-making process can still lead to a poor outcome, often due to circumstances beyond our control. We as leaders need to recognize threats posed by internal and external influential factors, which could be circumstantial or maybe nefarious "bad actors" with an ulterior motive driven by personal gain, jealousy, or explicit intent to undermine a project they choose not to support.

Heartbreaking as these events can be, often bruising our egos and potentially leading to future reluctance to "stick your neck out," you must reflect and remind yourself that you took the right path, made the right decisions, and yet there were unknown factors and potentially even bad actors at play that undermined your success. A situation that I know all too well, as I have personally witnessed and experienced many times throughout my career.

A recent and still emotionally scarring experience exemplifying this was a corporate sponsorship deal I had orchestrated with two of the biggest names in heavyweight boxing, on behalf of a blockchain-based non-fungible token (NFT) developer I was contracted to represent. The pair were scheduled to square off in a world championship bout, concluding what had become one of the greatest boxing trilogies of all time. It was a unicorn, once-in-a-career opportunity that would have provided unprecedented global exposure for my client's brand, generated enormous profits for each of the participating fighters, and created a first-of-its-kind blockchain use case for the sports industry.

Selfishly for me, it was the use case that I was most interested in, as it would have demonstrated the innovative strategies we were able to curate for our sports and entertainment clients.

Representing my client as the lead sponsor for one fighter, I personally negotiated the deal terms with his manager, a well-respected legend in the boxing community. A throwback personality, known as a man of his word and a consummate partner. It was these traits that, after receiving verbal approval from my client's CEO, he enthusiastically went on to share his excitement about our partnership, the innovative ideas we brought to the table, and that he would not consider any other offers even though we hadn't executed a formal contract yet. He then further shared that effective immediately his boxer and their entire support team would wear outfits emblazoned with my client's logo to press conferences, training sessions, and weigh-ins, an unprecedented promotional opportunity at the time. In addition, after we had signed contracts, my client would launch an innovative online NFT and digital asset storefront for each boxer that would provide them with a market-differentiating use case for the sports industry.

However, weeks after I had first received my CEO's approval on the deal terms, which were then memorialized within draft contracts and approved by each side's lawyers, I received a WhatsApp message late on a Thursday night that I will never forget. It was from my CEO, informing me that our company had established a new senior leadership team (SLT), unbeknownst to me and the rest of our executive team. This committee was led by an individual without the requisite experience or ownership stake and therefore did not have a vested interest in the company's success. As one of the SLT's first decisions, they chose to walk away from this deal even though it had already been approved in writing by our CEO. I felt like I'd been sucker-punched and dealt a devastating blow that could have long-term ramifications for both my reputation and that of our partners who'd worked so hard to pull this momentous deal together. Further, these executives showed no integrity or remorse for their actions, as they ceased all communications regarding the matter and refused to reimburse any of the expenses incurred by our partners.

It's in these types of scenarios where I have found true leaders emerge. Those individuals who recognize when ethical business practices have been compromised and, therefore, respond by taking a hard stance and choosing to do what is right, even if it meant short-term losses for themselves. Leading by example and demonstrating these qualities are what I have found to support our long-term career success, sustained personal relationships, and maintain our sense of personal integrity.

Recognizing my client's lack of contrition, I found myself in the painful scenario of having to deliver the unsavory news to each party, fully recognizing that this sudden change would cost each fighter tens of thousands in committed expenses and potentially millions in lost revenue. A jarring experience, particularly my conversation with the legendary manager who had given me his personal assurances and commitment to supporting "a mutually beneficial partnership." His response was simple and matter-of-fact: "At no point over the course of my entire career has someone walked away from a deal in this manner." Emphatically, he concluded our phone call by stating, "THIS IS NOT HOW BUSINESS IS DONE!" and then hung up the phone. To this day, my previous client has never attempted to reimburse any portion of the expenses committed. Neither I nor our partners has ever received an apology from the company I had represented.

What we can control is the reformation of a poor decision-making process that often has not provided the results we sought. If we are delusional and let our egos dominate our decisions, we mistakenly interpret poor outcomes as simply bad luck. While we might be aware of a significantly negative outcome, we might be unaware that it was the result of a bad decision-making process. In such cases, we learn nothing. With this mindset, we are doomed to repeat our mistakes. Self-reflective people are able to identify bad outcomes that have resulted from bad processes and see them as an opportunity to learn and avoid repeating their failures.

Having the opportunity to lead others, help individuals, and enable organizations to develop an openly collaborative and supportive culture has been a longtime goal of mine. Thank you for allowing me the opportunity to share my framework for *The Decision Switch* with you.

KNOW YOUR ROLE

When **People Work Together**
Great Things Happen

"Sometimes a player's greatest challenge is coming to grips with their role on the team."
—SCOTTIE PIPPEN

Before every decision, you need to ask yourself first, "What is my role?" It's a simple question that will have a profound effect on the amount of time and effort you devote to a decision, along with helping to clarify your level of responsibility and accountability. Clarity over your role, responsibilities, and authority are among the most crucial prerequisites of effective decision-making.

As owners, employees, and contractors, we often wear multiple hats and are required to perform jobs and tasks well outside of our defined job description. A practice that tends to create uncertainty and confusion amongst teams on who exactly is responsible for performing key roles in the decision-making process. Particularly in urgent situations where we find ourselves short on time, it's easy for small, but critical steps in a decision-making process to be overlooked. This is especially true when responsibilities for accomplishing those tasks are unclear. Less-desirable tasks are often overlooked because of a lack of interest, and, when left unchecked, are frequently forgotten.

Culture of Accountability

It's by having clearly articulated operational and leadership roles with well-defined responsibilities that we can begin to establish individualized expectations for all involved stakeholders. This level of clarity will help to cultivate a culture of accountability and mutual respect amongst peers, thereby having a profound effect on your organization and its ability to make nimble and effective decisions. It also serves to ensure no critical aspect of your decision-making process is overlooked. When roles and responsibilities are clearly defined, theoretically, no aspect is forgotten in the process.

I cannot emphasize enough that establishing a culture of account ability will cultivate a greater level of trust and camaraderie among your team and organization. It's human nature that we're more apt to develop stronger and more productive relationships when we know what to expect of others and, therefore, allow team members to concentrate on their respective responsibilities. When stakeholders are clear about their role in the process, you will find that it reduces competitive behaviors and counterproductive arguments that can delay or undermine the success of a desired outcome. Each example is an attribute of a dysfunctional organization fostering unproductive behaviors that consume precious time and energy that could have otherwise been focused on accomplishing the organization's goals and objectives.

Aligning Roles and Objectives

Throughout my career, I have often witnessed executives and key project stakeholders make decisions where they were ill-equipped or ill-informed to make an educated decision. This would often result in a failed project, program, or initiative. One such example is that of a former client of mine, then in desperate need of replacing their existing Human Resource (HR) management system. For myriad reasons, management had held on to their existing system for far too long despite it being antiquated, inefficient, and not meeting the organization's needs. After they had performed a much-needed system selection process, I acknowledged they had made a good and well-informed decision in choosing the best-in-class platform available at the time as their replacement.

My team was asked to assess the status and health of the replacement system's implementation and the potential risks posed to the organization. The reason for this was that our client had already invested more than seven years in design and development, incurred millions of dollars in license and consulting fees, and expended thousands of employee resource hours. As a reminder, my client still had not completed the implementation of the replacement HR system at the time we were asked to perform our review.

Likely initiated by the pressures of our pending assessment, a small group of executives held a meeting where they decided that after seven-plus years of investment and effort, they were going to pull the plug on the implementation. The reason provided publicly was that the HR system's technology and design had become outdated and ineffectively configured; therefore, it no longer met their needs. While I feel management's decision was the correct one, it resulted in a complete loss of funds invested, resource hours, and bruised stakeholders' political capital.

What could have caused such a catastrophe? There were a number of reasons, but the one I found most prominent was that the project management team had not taken the time to define responsibilities for critical roles, which created a litany of issues during the system's design and configuration.

As part of our postmortem review, I took the opportunity to interview several of the organization's executives. What I quickly discovered was that despite hiring multiple third-party system implementation firms to design and implement the new HR system, as well as align the underlying operational processes to be more efficient and effective, they had made a fatal error.

What was the leading culprit for the failed implementation? I found that there was a complete disconnect between the strategic intentions of the organization and the priorities of the individuals who were ultimately tasked with making critical technology and operational design decisions. Management's goals were to strengthen and streamline the organization's HR capabilities and operations, which would improve its overall performance and reduce the size of the operational support team. However, as a result of delegation, the people ultimately tasked with making critical design decisions were the same individuals responsible for performing the daily HR operational tasks.

As many of you can appreciate, these stakeholders did not want to voluntarily accept change. Many of them had been in their roles for years and were comfortable in their current position and unclear of management's goals and how the new system would impact their responsibilities. Due to a lack of communication from management, along with a lack of training and requisite knowledge, many feared the new HR system would require a change in responsibilities. In the worst of scenarios raised, it would eliminate the need for their position altogether.

As a result, the team made "safe" design decisions that resulted in configuring the new HR system to look and function exactly as the one they were replacing. The one thing that seems to be a global truth is that people are resistant to change, even if it is in the individual's or organization's best interest. Identifying the primary stakeholders who will be affected by the decisions you make and understanding their needs, will allow you to better understand the full ramifications of your choices and potentially dodge an easily avoidable mistake.

In this case, management failed to achieve its objectives of increasing productivity and reducing operational costs. The role responsible for the future state design of the HR department's management system had been incorrectly delegated. While an effective organizational leader, the HR officer accountable for the implementation was ill-equipped to oversee a technology program of this scope and magnitude, nor manage vendors they'd contracted with to assist with the system implementation, and, therefore, had delegated much of their responsibilities. The HR personnel making the final design decisions had not been briefed on the project's objectives or incentivized to consult with their contracted system implementation firms before making their recommendations. Ultimately, it was the system implementation firms that were held accountable for the failure, which, unfortunately, they could not have prevented.

This type of error is not uncommon and emphasizes the importance of role definition when making critical decisions. As the recipient of such a delegation, you are responsible for ensuring that you have the requisite knowledge, authority, and incentivization to accurately complete your task.

Advocacy versus Inquiry

It's worth noting that not all leaders approach decision-making in a way that produces the optimal outcome, especially as they pertain to allowing you to solicit and assess pertinent information and perspectives before coming to a conclusion. In the research performed by authors David A. Garvin and Michael A. Roberto, they identified that executives' processes typically fall underneath one of two broad approaches: advocacy and inquiry. [9]

Advocacy

Leaders who independently assess and make up their minds on what is the optimal decision, without taking into consideration the input and feedback others might provide, view advocacy-based decision-making as convincing and not collaborating. An activity with the purposeful intent of persuading others that they have made the right choice and therefore seeking to gain the necessary support required to push their agenda forward. In doing so, they share the upside of a decision, emphasizing the work and analysis performed, and why their conclusion was correct.

When multiple decision-makers are seeking to promote differing proposals or viewpoints, advocacy can devolve into a fractious stalemate causing division amongst key influencers and decision-makers. Potentially malicious behaviors manifest in various ways, examples of which are heated public debates or using subversive tactics, such as sidebar discussions and political leverage, to undermine their opponent and promote their position. It's in these types of instances that we find debating parties often purposely withhold pertinent risks and potentially damaging details related to their proposal and embellish the positive aspects of their analysis and anticipated outcome.

For example, leaders focused on their own needs, say two executives from dueling sales divisions submitting self-serving budget requests. Each budget provides their division an ample increase for new headcount to help sustain, if not drive revenue growth. In doing so, they proceed to advocate solely based on their division's needs and not taking into consideration those of other departments and the broader organization's goals. This example exemplifies a missed opportunity for executive colleagues to understand, collaborate, and prioritize the needs of every division, which could have produced innovative ideas that addressed their individual needs as well as supported the organization's overall mission in a more impactful and cost-effective manner. It is in these types of dilemmas that leaders will frequently lose their ability to remain objective and listen to the opinions of others, all due to their fixation on winning and gaining the approval they so desire. As in the case of the aforementioned sales executives, they might choose to stymie the voices of opposing positions for fear that they might jeopardize their chances of attaining the additional budget and resources requested.

This is a trait I've often found prevalent within startups and private partnerships, particularly as it relates to annual performance reviews and partnership promotion processes—the results of which directly impact an individual's career trajectory and annual compensation package. Processes that are often perpetuated and perceived as a formal evaluation used to assess and categorize an individual's performance and their contribution to the practice. This promotes the optics of transparency and inclusion of the opinions made by its managers and directors. The real truth is most critical decisions are made by a select few individuals, typically highly influential founders and partners using frequently subjective criteria.

Inquiry

Leaders who take an inquiry-based approach to decision-making actively seek out the views, inputs, and opinions of others. They understand that while they might have a valid point of view, they also recognize the success of a decision frequently relies on the quality that comes from having made informed choices that have been shaped by pertinent data points, key influencers, and vested stakeholders. Similarly to advocacy, they seek to gain the necessary support of others to achieve a desired outcome; however, they don't come to the table selling an idea but asking for objective feedback on how to make it even better. Inherently, stakeholders who have been provided an opportunity to contribute and help shape a decision are vastly more invested in its success, and, therefore, more likely to support the final conclusion.

Often, I have found leaders in these situations confidently recognize their limitations and choose to actively initiate discourse with other key stakeholders and knowledgeable experts in their pursuit of a desired outcome. In doing so, they openly share information, requesting critical and objective feedback on the analysis performed and decision recommendations. While discussions might become contentious, these types of disagreements are beneficial to the process. Participants understand that it's not personal and tend to become actively engaged in the debate and ultimately vested in identifying and supporting the optimal decision. It's by cultivating an open and supportive culture that participants feel comfortable in making their conclusions independently, based on their own assessment, which provides the opportunity to uncover additional options that might better serve the organization.

Garvin and Roberto concluded the two contrasting views of advocacy versus inquiry as, "Leaders who seek to improve their organizations' decision-making capabilities need to begin with a single goal: shifting from an advocacy-influenced decision-making process to one of inquiry. Reframing decisions in this manner will help to cut through the noise and distractions created by competing positions, thereby allowing you to focus on what is really within your purview."[10]

PRINCIPLE 1:
TRIAGE FIRST

Increase Your Productivity by **Assessing and Prioritizing** before Taking Action

"Knowing what you don't know is more useful than being brilliant."
— CHARLES THOMAS MUNGER

Have you ever responded to an email or question before you fully understood and digested the information provided, only to realize afterward (embarrassingly) that you misread the request and made the wrong decision? If you're like 99 percent of us, the answer is yes.

Why is this the case and what is the root cause? More than likely, it's the result of multitasking, inadequate prioritization, or potentially, decision fatigue. We live in a fluid state of decision-making, requiring us to continuously consume and analyze information, but as humans, we are prone to errors. Putting this into perspective, think for a moment about the role of an air-traffic controller whose sole responsibility is to monitor a constant barrage of information provided by their computer systems, colleagues, communication platforms, and sometimes even still by sight. This is a critical role in today's global transportation system, as the slightest mistake might result in the deaths of hundreds of passengers. Recognizing the potential risks an error might create and the benefits provided by openly sharing flight status and conditions-related information, the Federal Aviation Administration implemented the Collaborative Decision Making initiative to improve, "...air traffic flow management through increased information exchange among aviation community stakeholders."[11]

In the long term, the result of consistently making poor decisions with negative results will limit your career growth and will ultimately undermine your credibility and social currency. Successful leaders learn to quickly triage a decision request and evaluate if they have sufficient information to proceed. If there are gaps in the information provided, they immediately request clarification or additional information.

The term "triage" is derived from the French word "trier" meaning "to separate items according to quality" and was initially used for sorting food products such as coffee. It is believed to have been first used in the field of medicine during World War I. The triage process consisted of first assessing a patient's condition and then sorting by the level of severity, prioritizing those with the most life-threatening but still treatable cases. Triage stayed in the international medical lexicon and is still widely used. Today, triage, or the designation of degrees of urgency, is a medical term used within a hospital's emergency room to determine the prognosis, criticality, time, and effort required to treat ailing patients. Based on these inputs, medical staff are able to more effectively manage, prioritize, and ultimately deliver the greatest amount of medical care or "value" to their patient population.

A foundational concept taught in medical and nursing schools, the the triage methodology protocol is taught to health care professionals so that patients with the most serious conditions receive attention first. Every health care organization I have worked with has resource and capacity limitations, and when faced with a sudden influx of new cases necessitates the prioritization of care and resources for those patients who most urgently require it. Patient care prioritization, like decision-making, is never a static task but a continuous process that evolves over time based on changes to the environment that include staffing, adverse events, or the admittance of new patients.

In nursing, the pressure to continuously make critical choices is called decision fatigue, and the process of triage has been developed to aggregate and prioritize what really matters. Fortunately, in the world of business, we are usually not required to make life-or-death decisions. However, the concept provides the same fundamental value as it does in medicine: prioritizing decisions based on a request's criticality, time sensitivity, or value. Unfortunately, triage is not a concept often taught outside of health care. Recognizing when you have been prompted to make a decision is only the first step in the assessment process. Triage requires dedicating the necessary time to understand what you have been asked so that you can effectively respond with the requisite sense of urgency. To do this, I have found the following three-gate evaluation model to be particularly effective.

- **Knowledge Confirmation:** Do I understand what is being asked of me? Am I the right person to respond to the request? Do I have all the necessary information to competently respond? Often when presented with a decision, we are provided with an incomplete situational assessment, background information, or dataset. It is in these instances where you as the leader need to assess whether you have sufficient knowledge and understanding to make an informed decision or if the situation calls for immediate action.

- **Criticality:** Have I assessed the criticality of the decision, dependencies, time constraints, or justifiable deadline for my response? In many cases, we are prompted with a decision request that might not include a clear definition of urgency, or, more simply, a deadline. In these instances, how can we properly triage a decision and determine its criticality? Regardless of knowing what the deadline is, it is crucial for you to understand the driving forces behind the timing of the request.

- **Value Proposition:** What is the value of my decision, and does it take precedence over other alternative actions? If you are like me, you have more requests and commitments than you have time in the day to respond. In these scenarios, as a leader, you need to prioritize the decisions that will provide the greatest value after taking into account the first two gates.

Personal Aside

Early in my career, I recall having an innate need to be the first to respond to a request or question. I had a false belief that responding quickly would earn me accolades or a reward. What I did not realize at the time was that responding quickly, but incorrectly, only magnified the negative recourse I would receive.

I quickly learned that responding correctly is vastly more important than responding quickly. Fortunately, I had several mentors over my career who recognized this development opportunity and provided me with the necessary direction. The first was at Sempra Energy, my first job out of college. The vice president (VP) whom I reported to sat me down after my first couple of weeks on the job to discuss the implications of error in one's decision-making. In my role as an associate, I was responsible for documenting and reconciling the trade details for West Texas Intermediate crude oil derivative swaps, often valued in excess of $50 million. The slightest error could have significant financial or regulatory consequences for the firm, so accuracy was vastly more important than speed.

To this day, I vividly recall the following coaching this VP gave me. He shared, "The first time I have to question or need to correct one of your decisions, I will take fault for not properly educating or explaining the request. The second time I will interpret that you are not listening or thinking and begin to question your competence. The third time I find your response is off-point or incorrect, you will be fired."

Message received. In case you were wondering, I never found myself needing a third correction and only required a second clarification on a handful of occasions.

Time and again, I see both new hires and experienced managers who do not prioritize decision-making and choose to "wing it." Over the course of your life, career success and personal fulfillment will likely be attributed to a handful of key decisions. Your challenge is trying to identify when you are being presented with one of those critical decisions. Properly triaging a decision will enable you to recognize the size, scale, and effort required to address an event. Lack of concern about a decision can generally be attributed to either being overtasked in your role or simply ambivalent over the decision's outcome. Both are inexcusable. Each is a clear sign that you are not effectively managing your time or areas of responsibility as a present or future leader. Worse, you have become an impediment to the organization's success in meeting its objectives and goals.

Later in my career, I was fortunate to report to one of my firm's national client service partners who was responsible for the delivery of professional services to several of the largest health care organizations in the United States. As the client service director overseeing the delivery of professional services at several of this partner's accounts, I was responsible for the day-to-day client and operations management. Early in our relationship, I observed this partner frequently review an email or text, which requested a decision or answer, and they would not respond then—or maybe at all. At the time, this seemed counterintuitive to the nature of client service, and I often wondered why they proceeded in this fashion. Would it not be more efficient to resolve a decision immediately and move forward? As time passed, I admittedly found myself on the receiving end of similar treatment. Having requested what I believed were critical and time-sensitive decisions, I would often receive an incomplete response and sometimes none at all.

As part of one feedback session, I asked the partner a point-blank question about his approach to decision-making and responding to inquiries. Caught off guard by the directness of my inquiry, his response was simple and would forever change how I approached decision-making. Coming into the discussion, I had treated decisions like an inventory management model, "first in, first out." This meant that I would address requests in a sequential manner, to be sure no request went unfulfilled. When pressed for his approach, the partner simply said that he responded only to those that required his immediate attention. To do this, he scanned emails or texts, intuitively prioritizing when, and if, he would respond based on the gates mentioned above. Otherwise, he left it to the director or the director's team to resolve the request or make a critical decision. While his approach lacked tact, I have to admit it was effective.

Despite the exceptional volume of decisions required of a partner on a daily basis, there was only a finite amount of time they were able to commit to assessing and making a decision. As a result, it was imperative they address those most urgently requiring action and leave the unanswered decisions to resolve themselves. As a young executive, I observed and adopted the same thought process, where I learned to quickly assess the criticality, time, and effort required for a decision. This wound up being infinitely helpful with time management through learning to assess and prioritize my own decisions but also filtering what I would escalate to management.

Similar to the world of consulting, I have observed that virtually every industry has uniquely defined triggers that shift how critical decisions are recategorized and therefore managed through an expedited and abbreviated process. These triggers might be tied to a sales organization's revenue target or a software development firm's patch release schedule. In each of these scenarios, the organization has an optional secondary process composed of a subset of the standard evaluation protocols, frequently bypassing critical steps, in an effort to achieve a desired goal. When used appropriately, critical decisions will justifiably take precedence over competing priorities, enabling the requestor to achieve a desired outcome. However, if misused and allowing "bad actors" to take advantage of the reduced controls and protocols used to evaluate a decision, an increased number of errors will frequently result. These errors are a result of bypassing critical steps in their standard processes, such as information gathering or quality review.

A very real risk for large and complex organizations that have implemented rigid and rigorous approval processes is allowing urgent decisions to receive preferential treatment and to be fast-tracked, effectively reducing the level of due diligence and analysis typically performed. Once a self-serving leader or department discovers this loophole, they are inherently incentivized to circumvent the standard processes and designate a decision as urgent for potentially ulterior motives, such as requests that are politically charged, those that lack the requisite research and analysis, or a decision approval tied to a deadline where the request was simply overlooked and therefore submitted late. When a disproportional percentage of decisions are designated as a high priority, the end result is almost always a decline in quality and thoughtfulness in making the optimal choice. For example, a software development team with an upcoming product release might elect to circumvent critical steps in the quality review process to meet a symbolic date set by an uniformed client executive.

The reason for this is that when every decision becomes rushed, the individuals responsible for analyzing and assessing approval requests become overburdened and fatigued, due to the pressures created by constantly "hitting" the urgency button. This creates a greater opportunity for flaws and errors to be overlooked, which the rigors of their standard review process would have flagged. Effective screening of a decision's priority starts at the top and requires mindfully defining objective criteria used to qualify levels of urgency and which decisions truly need to be fast-tracked versus those that can run through normal processes.

Your takeaway? If you're like most people, you have a to-do list a mile long. It is impossible to give 100 percent of your attention to the thousands of decisions you are presented with on a daily basis. Learning to prioritize tasks based on their criticality, time, and effort required is the first step in learning how to make better decisions for both oneself and the company as a whole. Understanding the importance of triage as it relates to prioritization allows you as the decision-maker to reorder your to-be-completed tasks by precedence. In other words, identify urgent tasks with short reaction timelines and those that have future deadlines or can wait until after all your urgent tasks have been completed. This is where mastery of triage comes in.

📝 Self-Study Questions:

- Is this a decision I need to make now, in the future, or at all?
- How urgent is this decision and what factors are contributing to this timeline, and are there dependencies I need to be aware of?
- Did I fully read/listen/understand the decision presented to me? Or have I rushed through the information-gathering process?
- Do I have all information necessary to conclude? For the sake of completeness, have I inquired if there were other pertinent data points available? Or did I unintentionally assume I had all the necessary information available?
- In an urgent scenario, when asked to expedite a decision without all the facts, have I disclosed that portions of the requisite information were not available?

PRINCIPLE 2:
FOLLOW YOUR NORTH STAR

Defining a Clear Objective Serves to Align All Subsequent Decisions

"Our North Star has always been the same, which for us is about making insanely great products that really change the world in some way—enrich people's lives."
—TIM COOK

When faced with a critical choice, how often do you take into consideration whether that decision aligns with your ultimate objective or North Star, which could be a personal goal, an organization's mission statement, or even an entrepreneurial aspiration? "North Star" is a phrase often prophesied by Steve Jobs' close friend and successor, Tim Cook. Without a qualm, Cook frequently and clearly asserts Apple's objective wasn't to be first but to be the best. Having the fortune of living through the birth and evolution of Apple's success, as I reflect on its product development history there are few instances where they were the first. More often, they elevated the functionality, design, and utility of technologies, products, and solutions already in existence. To name but a few, storing and transporting music, integrating cameras within our portable phones, and optimizing the design of wireless headphones. Bottom line, before making every critical decision you need to ask yourself if it will propel you forward in achieving a desired outcome, or if it will compromise your progress for the sake of an alternate goal, such as vanity or self-promotion.

A North Star represents an unwavering definition of your purpose, objective, or goal. Greg Shepherd, a serial entrepreneur and contributor to the Chief Executive newsletter explains, "When CEOs begin building their businesses without establishing a North Star, they risk traveling in directions that won't yield the desired outcomes—and, in many cases, they don't realize it until it's too late to correct the course."[12]

Defining your North Star often proves to be the most critical stage of decision-making, as it provides the foundational roots and direction for virtually all subsequent actions. Developing your North Star can be a time-intensive process requiring you to objectively assess what you stand for and what your purpose is, and only then distill that vision into a simple and clear statement.

Personally, my North Star is "family first." When faced with a challenging decision, I have found this to be a calming recalibration reference to ensure my choices are rooted in the personal values and goals I have established. When prompted to explain what family first means to me, I envision a healthy and loving relationship with my wife and daughters in which we could always rely on and make meaningful time for each other. Throughout my personal life, my career, and even at this very moment, I am making decisions and taking risks that align with my North Star.

In a business setting with many stakeholders, defining your North Star is critical to ensuring success and achieving an intended outcome on the most efficient and effective path available. Due to the increasing complexity of the business world today, leaders often are faced with numerous distractions, or false North Stars that are rooted within tangential financial, operational, or regulatory drivers. In these times, I have often witnessed leaders who, due to lack of clarity, have made decisions that were counterproductive or ultimately did not progress the organization toward its intended objectives.

Symbolism

The North Star is a common reference to Polaris, an actual star located essentially straight above the Earth's North Pole. Visible from any point in the northern hemisphere, the closer you get to the North Pole the higher it sits in the sky. Polaris' notoriety stems from its stationary presence in the sky, where its location is aligned with our planet's rotational axis. So no matter what time, day, or season the Earth rotates around this fixed point, like a spinning top.

An incredibly powerful example of the North Star metaphor comes from the Polynesians, an indigenous tribe who for thousands of years have inhabited the South Sea Islands of the broader Oceania region in the Pacific Ocean. This region spans nearly forty million square miles and is composed of thousands of islands, many of which are extremely remote. Using simple dugout canoes, the Polynesians would complete voyages over thousands of miles of open ocean waters, primarily using their knowledge of the stars and constellations to guide them. Despite facing a multitude of risks, challenges, and disruptions, they were able to successfully navigate the open sea of the South Pacific. Similar to our personal and professional lives, the Polynesians knew how to set a course and tactically navigate through obstacles such as storms and vigorous currents. By maintaining their focus on the ultimate objective, or North Star, they made the requisite decisions necessary to complete their voyage.

Having a long and rich history in assisting travelers to navigate the globe, the term North Star evolved into a symbol for our goals, objectives, and personal growth. Just as the North Star provided mariners and explorers with a steady beacon in the sky to guide and help them stay on course, so does our own North Star. For each of us, it's a unique ambition or objective that reflects our intentions, aspirations, and values.

Psychologist and best-selling author Rick Hanson, PhD, has noted that, "When you find your North Star, you know where you're headed. That alone feels good. Plus, your North Star is (presumably) wholesome and vital, so aiming toward it will bring more and more happiness and benefit to yourself and others. And you can dream bigger dreams and take more chances in life since if you lose your way, you've got a beacon to home in on." [13]

In a corporate setting, establishing a North Star that best captures your goals, core values, or mission, will help to simplify the decision-making process, leading to improved results and better outcomes. This is due to the establishment of a common objective that grounds all stakeholders and thereby reduces the time or needs to collectively discuss decisions that your North Star will address. Defining your North Star serves three critical purposes:

1. It helps prioritize and accelerate informed, yet decentralized, decision-making.
2. It helps teams align stakeholders and streamline communications.
3. It enables your teams to focus on the defined goal and assess the value or impact a decision will have on your ability to achieve that goal.

One of the great examples where I have personally witnessed the North Star concept applied in business involves a previous client of mine. They are a not-for-profit health insurance company focused on the senior segment of our population, and whose stated mission is, "Keeping Seniors Healthy and Independent." Building upon this vision, their leaders created a powerful mantra many years ago that is still used today to guide virtually every administrative purchasing decision.

Why? The answer is twofold. Their members are aging adults, often living on fixed incomes and, therefore, sensitive to price increases on standard household expenses such as health insurance. In addition, their members were frequently prone to medical conditions that required significant financial support. As a result, their leadership team recognized that for them to stay competitive in the market, they had to get lean on administrative costs.

It was with this clarity that their leaders added one simple yet specific question to ask when deciding whether to approve a purchase. That question: "Would a dollar spent on this program provide more benefit to our members than simply handing it back to them?" While not always easy to objectively measure, it benefitted the decision-making process by placing a subjective lens on a request that required their leaders to be thoughtful with their approval decision and able to defend their conclusion.

In my ten years serving this client, I worked with many of their executive leaders on topics such as technology, process improvement, and regulatory compliance. At the end of each project, my firm would provide a final report to management summarizing our observations and recommendations for improvement. It was enlightening to witness firsthand how powerful this simple question was in aligning their leader's decisions. In their evaluation of our recommendations and whether to proceed, if the answer to this one simple question was no, or even uncertain, it was turned down.

Defining Your North Star

As a result of our upbringing, teachings, and mentors, we have developed our own personal internal compass. This helps us to define our purpose and beliefs. Additionally, our personal North Star helps to shape how we view the objectives of a given decision or project, and whether it was successfully achieved. In many cases, defining your North Star is the most personal and conflicting stage in your decision-making process.

Successful leaders are able to separate the critical elements of a decision from background noise associated with personal or political ambitions, to identify the decision that best aligns with the organization's goals. A challenge for many, as it requires you to deliberately take the time to turn inward and identify who you are, what you believe in, what you stand for, and why. Upon reflection, I have found that many managers do not take the time to articulate their personal principles, speaking instead on behalf of the organization as a whole. Yet, for the individual responsible for making a decision, if their view of an organization's North Star is skewed by their personal views and values, it can have a significant impact on the final determination.

Not Always One North Star

An obvious characteristic of a North Star is that it features only one goal, objective, or mission. What happens when you have multiple teams, departments, or projects, each performing different functions? Certainly, larger enterprises with multiple divisions and different product management, product development departments, and customer bases might have different North Stars tied to that group's goal, objective, or mission.

In these cases, I have found it effective to align teams based on a common and measurable goal, such as profitability, quality, or a production deadline, that will help to keep everyone focused on the same objective. This will assist you in aligning stakeholders and cultivating a culture of collaboration. When teams fail to connect their North Star to an organization's goal or objective, they run the risk of leading their business down the wrong path.

At a personal level, you might have also defined multiple North Stars that have evolved over time. Early in my career, I had parallel ambitions to become a consultant as well as a college professor. As I saw it, the connective tissue between the two was the notion of giving back by sharing knowledge. Recognizing my limited amount of experience, I purposely staggered these North Stars to allow for my personal development in the world of consulting and vision that it would better prepare me to one day take on the role of a college professor. As a result, I followed my initial North Star into the world of corporate consulting and trusted that my vision of one day becoming a professor would guide me in the direction necessary to accomplish my goal.

Solution-Focused

I have found one key attribute that separates successful leaders and organizations—their ability to identify and focus on an outcome or solution, while not getting stuck on a particular issue or roadblock. Solution-led leaders believe their surest path to accomplishing their goals comes as a result of proactively identifying potential problems that might derail the outcome of a decision and identifying opportunities to mitigate, if not resolve an issue. A solution-led organization optimizes team structures, cross-department collaboration, communication channels, and other processes to ensure the success of its objective.

Illustrating this, it was during an offhand conversation with an industrial lighting manufacturing client's head of marketing that I saw firsthand the power and value of solution-focused leadership. As background, the company's product line historically ranged from simple handheld flashlights to large lighting towers often seen at construction worksites. Integrated within their sales and marketing strategy they had purposely defined themselves as an illumination solutions provider. A distinction that served them well in convincing wholesale customers and private label resellers of the organization's objective and brand value.

Seeking to broaden their product offering, he'd collaborated with their product development team to create a new line of safety products that incorporated lighting into the traditional reflective materials used in vests and helmets. Finding this to be a brilliant innovation and a fan of market disruption, I couldn't help but ask him how the new product line was performing. Surprisingly, he shared they were struggling as he'd found their sales team had simply folded the new products into their existing portfolio of illumination solutions. Therefore, customers saw them as an inexperienced manufacturer playing outside of their wheelhouse, rather than as an industry-leading innovator seeking to apply their expertise and create solutions meant to save the lives of professionals working in hazardous conditions, such as road construction crews working the night shift. It was with this revelation that he pivoted the new product line's sales and marketing strategy and began targeting customers seeking innovative opportunities to protect their employees, as well as reduce the legal liabilities associated with preventable fatalities.

Calling an organization "solution-led" does not mean that one leader or department will always resolve any relevant issues, but that the company as a whole will do so through a collaborative approach to problem-solving. Anyone can identify a problem, but it takes a leader to truly consider all aspects of a given situation and develop an appropriate solution to address the identified issue.

Unique

As a general rule, I suggest developing a North Star that is unique to your particular goal, objective, and mission. I advise tailoring the descriptive language used to reflect the culture, nomenclature, or individuality of the person or organization who authored it, as well as their passion, strategy, or mission. Incorporating what makes your North Star unique will create a greater sense of ownership and responsibility.

However, there are often instances where your mission and North Star are not particularly unique or differentiated. That is perfectly acceptable. Don't worry if your North Star might not feel particularly unique, as individuals and organizations frequently have similar objectives. Think for a moment about global brands such as Amazon, about whom it would be easy to assume that there are scores of organizations with similar goals due to the breadth of their product and service offerings. Aside from Amazon's goal of being the lowest cost provider, they have incorporated contextualized differentiators such as industry-leading fulfillment cycle times, as well as a flexible and generous return management process.

Understandable

Your North Star should be a simple and easily understood description of your goal. It should be an assertion where the language and terminology used to articulate your objective are clear, concise, and framed in a manner that someone unfamiliar with the industry, discipline, or activity is able to grasp the concept and what you seek to achieve. This is a lesson I learned early in my consulting career.

Having completed a complex cybersecurity assessment for a religious-based health care system, our team was in the process of preparing the final report for their board of directors. The composition of the board included community leaders, executives from the health care system, and representatives of the founding religious organization. In typical fashion, our report would provide an overview of the procedures performed, issues identified, and ultimately our recommendations on how to resolve the critical risks we had uncovered. As with many of our clients, their executives had become accustomed to incorporating our suggestions within the goals of the division we had assessed.

After having reviewed the initial draft report, our partner pulled me aside to provide candid feedback on the language and recommendations we had drafted. While recognizing the technical nature of the work, he simply asked me if I felt someone with a secular or religious education would understand our recommendations. The example used to make an emphatic point related to the technical standards we had recommended for configuring their network perimeter firewalls. I was struck with an epiphany. The value of our services was dependent on their board's ability to understand the associated risks and our recommendations so they could incorporate them within their goals and hold leaders accountable for achieving a desired result. In this case, the concept, description, and language would have baffled anyone without a computer science degree.

He then provided me with a simple question to ask myself when preparing a client deliverable, essentially functioning as a litmus test for the language we would use. "Would your parents, or in this case a Catholic nun, be able to understand the risks and your recommendations?" If not, you need to reassess and simplify the language used.

Measurable

The last and often most critical aspect of defining your North Star is to ensure that it is measurable. This is a function that is dependent on your objective, whether that is to improve the performance of a perpetual task or the completion of a discrete project within a predetermined time frame.

Utilizing the aforementioned examples, Amazon's goals for fulfillment times would be best measured using key performance indicators (KPIs), as it is a perpetual function. Active monitoring of real-time results using KPIs, as well as benchmarking against historical performance levels enables you to quickly identify and address issues as they arise. In the case of the health care system, their objective was to document organizational standards for their network firewalls and then update corresponding hardware configurations. Each is a discrete goal, composed of subtasks that can be tracked to ensure their successful completion within the defined timeframes. Project tracking is an effective approach for measuring progress, as delays and obstacles can be easily identified, escalated, and resolved.

In each case, your ability to measure performance is a crucial aspect of the North Star you have defined. As your North Star, finding that a perpetual activity is underperforming or finding a discrete goal behind schedule, provides the opportunity to assess impediments that need to be addressed or competing priorities that should be considered in evaluating whether to take action.

A North Star that succinctly captures your objective serves to establish mental guardrails that focus your attention, actions, and aligns all subsequent decisions. It therefore allows you to avoid the "drift" that frequently undermines a successful outcome to your decisions as a result of unconscious distractions, competing priorities, and contrary opinions of influential stakeholders.

📝 Self-Study Questions:

- Have I/we defined an objective in simple, clear, and concise terms, so that others are able to understand and can follow?
- Does my decision align with the ultimate objective I seek to achieve?
- What are the laws and/or ethical considerations impacting this decision?
- Are there policies or precedents that I need to consider in my conclusion? What is the intent of those policies?

PRINCIPLE 3:
COLLABORATE WITH OTHERS

The Power of Numbers in
Achieving Your Goals

"The most important single ingredient in the formula of success is knowing how to get along with people."
—THEODORE ROOSEVELT

Have you ever spent days, weeks, or even months working on a presentation you believed fully captured every angle, each minute detail, and anticipated that it would be well embraced by your intended audience, only to find your proposition, analysis, and recommendations are challenged, discounted, or maybe even disregarded? If you are like me, you have had a similar outcome occur at least a few times over your professional life.

Why?

Did you take into consideration whether it was your decision alone or whether there were other stakeholders who had a vested interest or would be impacted, and, therefore, should have been consulted? In advance of your presentation, had you shared your analysis and recommendations with influential members of your audience or did you simply ask them to confirm your final conclusion? Or, even if it was your decision alone, should you have cultivated a broader coalition of support to amplify the notion of consensus and support for your decision prior to making a public announcement?

Making a well-informed decision requires you to take an intentional and inclusive approach to seek out and obtain relevant information, opinions, and perspectives from a broad and diverse group of supporters, opposers, and those who simply have a view of the situation. Gaining insights and assessing alternative options, will serve to help shape the view of a situation and assist in selecting the optimal decision available. This approach will take more time, and, therefore, put most of us off, as we all have the desire to address and solve a problem as quickly as possible. However, I have frequently found that poor decisions came as a result of a leader who chose to take a shortsighted and incomplete approach to the triage and discovery processes, therefore limiting the information and options available to consider before making a final decision. Taking the time to explore an expanded set of options provides the opportunity to uncover a breakthrough approach.

Particularly in the case of significant decisions, I find it essential to engage individuals who might be influential to your success, those who will be directly responsible for carrying out the subsequent activities, as well as those who will be held accountable for the personnel or departments impacted. Additionally, taking into consideration alternative or even contradictory points of view from key stakeholders prior to making a decision will provide objective perspectives to help ensure your success. Lastly, for public or politically charged decisions, taking the time to educate and share your ideas with influential stakeholders prior to making a public announcement will help to ensure the ultimate decision will be successful and well received.

Human Design

Whether you are delivering a presentation at a board of directors meeting or the results of a decision you made at a department meeting, soliciting preliminary input, feedback, and support will dramatically increase the success rate on how your decisions are received by others. Leaders who proactively seek differing opinions are much more likely to come to a well-rounded conclusion that considers the impact a decision might have on them and their business. In addition, seeking to inform and request support prior to going into a proposal reduces the surprise factor that often undermines the success of a decision, while helping to build momentum among those you have included in the process. Some leaders might shy away from requesting external input on a decision to avoid additional complexity or the potential of a contrary opinion. Harvard Business School Online's Matt Garvin comments, "Yet the ideas that could come out of a collaborative conversation are often far more valuable and critical to a decision's success." [14]

Generally speaking, business leaders, particularly those who are type-A executives, inherently want the opportunity to participate in the decision-making process, contribute their input and perspectives, and confirm their voices have been heard. An often-obvious example of this is an organization's chief financial officer (CFO), whose primary role is to oversee the company's financial operations. Often an influential role, I distinctly recall a software development client whose CFO had captivated the attention and trust of their executive leadership team. Time and time again, I found the success rate for virtually any request for a capital project approval directly correlated to the CFO's level of awareness and, in certain cases, their direct involvement in the development of the proposal. When the time comes to deliver an executive committee presentation or resource request, you are far more likely to achieve a successful outcome if you invest the time beforehand to educate and share with key stakeholders.

The reason for this is twofold. The first is public participation. This is the idea that better decisions come from having a rich and diverse dataset that is founded on facts and not just one person's opinion. The second is psychology, in this instance, anger, fear, and human insecurity. In the competitive nature of business, no one wants to look foolish, surprised, or unprepared in a public forum. In these situations, uninformed executives who are asked to approve or support a critical decision, particularly in front of an audience, are far more likely to turn it down for fear of making the wrong decision.

Public Participation

Public decisions made in a collaborative manner that invites and incorporates stakeholders' input on the front end are generally more durable, last longer, and are more likely to result in a successful outcome. Engaging these individuals early—maybe even in the triage phase—can have a dramatic impact on your ability to advance a decision, simply by providing more information, greater transparency, and a richer understanding of the topic, as well as the reasoning why the decision presented was the optimal choice. As defined by Jody Horntvedt, a professor at the University of Minnesota, three of the primary reasons for this are as follows:[15]

- **More information:** "[Stakeholder] involvement brings more information to the decision, including scientific or technical knowledge, knowledge about the context where decisions are implemented, institutions involved, history, and personalities. More information can make the difference between a good and a poor decision."
- **More perspectives:** "Additional perspectives expand options and enhance the value of the ultimate decision. The more

views you gather in the process of making a decision, the more likely your final choice will meet the most needs and address the most concerns possible."

- **Increased mutual understanding:** "Public participation provides a forum for decision-makers and stakeholders to understand each others' issues and viewpoints. The discussions broaden the knowledge base as each one contributes to the decision."

Psychology

I have found that we need to thoughtfully evaluate whether to propose a decision in a public forum, particularly those ideas that are complex or political and have the potential of receiving a negative reaction. As Allison Pickens of The New Normal Fund shares, "A good rule of thumb is if you're anticipating conflict, give people a chance to think about the topic well ahead of time."[16] With this in mind, I strongly recommend that you avoid surprising an audience with a controversial subject with the expectation that they will be ready to discuss it right away. This approach is frequently met with a cautious, if not a dissenting response that amplifies the negative conjecture, as a result of the group setting. Further, Allison Pickens goes on to explain that "some folks are internal processors and they need time to think on their own."

It's for this reason that I suggest socializing new concepts and recommendations with key executives before making a public announcement or management presentation. Taking the time to educate and familiarize influential executives will cultivate trust and more productive meeting discussions, resulting in better decisions that inherently receive broader support for the outcomes you seek to achieve. The reason for this is self-preservation and the natural human instinct to protect ourselves, and that includes our reputations. Rather than making a rash and uninformed decision, leaders are far more likely to defer judgment or simply reject a proposal on the spot. While the requestor initially leaves with a bruised ego, the real impact is a damaged reputation.

To be explicitly frank with you, putting an executive unexpectedly on the spot in front of their peers makes you a dangerous threat. Surprising a group of executives with a politically charged and contentious decision serves to call into question your judgment, your ability to attract others to follow, and ultimately your ability to be an effective and trusted leader. In my experience, either scenario often proves to be a career-limiting decision. Trust is a foundational attribute of a productive relationship and without it, you are a liability to your peers and an unpredictable variable for the organization. In these situations, it's human instinct to mitigate, if not eliminate, unnecessary risk and uncertainty.

By recognizing this human condition and therefore incorporating the requisite time to educate and collaborate with your audience before making an announcement or management presentation, you will dramatically increase the likelihood of receiving executive support and approval, therefore, contributing to your personal and professional success.

Additionally, it should be noted that proactive collaboration helps to neutralize many negative management practices, such as social undermining and bottom-line mentality. These types of negative initiatives, behaviors, or feelings are often unrelated to your decision and often rooted in self-interest or the act of protecting one's position, power, or initiative.

- **Social undermining:** The conscious and intentional actions of a "bad actor," generally rooted in envy, seeking to challenge if not derail an individual or project from accomplishing its objective. As an instrumental form of aggression, social undermining behaviors (e.g., belittling, gossiping, withholding information, or giving someone "the silent treatment") are powerful ways to bolster oneself at others' expense. Because the negative effects of undermining are cumulative and often grow more deleterious over time, it is reasonable to expect those envious individuals will use this form of moral disengagement.

- **Bottom-line mentality:** The mindset of leaders who manage solely based on financial performance goals and therefore often neglect competing priorities such as a company's growth strategy, mission statement, values, ethics, and employee well-being. Leaders with a bottom-line mentality often serve as poor collaborative partners, due to an unwavering focus on improving financial results, thereby overlooking or consciously disregarding other organizational priorities.

In both cases, the practice of proactively collaborating provides the opportunity to better understand the position of other influential stakeholders. Collaborating and socializing ideas before a meeting allows an individual to contribute to the final outcome; therefore, reducing the potential for social undermining, increasing the likelihood of partnering, and soliciting their support. In the case of bottom-line mentality, proactive collaboration provides the opportunity to define and align the criteria used to evaluate a particular decision or initiative. Providing others the ability to contribute toward metrics that will be used to evaluate a decision will yield clarity on how they value your proposal, while also allowing you to educate them on the value proposition and additional metrics they should consider.

Expect the Unexpected

Incorporating feedback from a variety of sources might impact our decisions in ways you might not have expected or may have potentially taken for granted. As but one example, in 1904, the American tea trader Thomas Sullivan shipped samples to his customers in small silk bags, for transportation purposes only. However, when they were received, customers assumed the bags were to be used like the metal infusers that were common at the time, and, therefore, put the tea bags into hot water.

Though Sullivan didn't come up with the idea, he was able to find value in his customers' mistake, even taking steps to improve the effect and develop sachets made of gauze. Tea bags were invented, and Sullivan's sales skyrocketed.

It's important to recognize that sometimes the best ideas might not come from the most obvious source or expert on a given topic. Sometimes the best solutions come from an unexpected source. Opening up the decision-making process to others can lead to serendipitous solutions and better outcomes. By incorporating the views of stakeholders representing varied and diverse backgrounds, roles, experience, or expertise to participate in your decision-making process, you are more apt to discover a solution you might not have otherwise considered. And that's great, particularly when an idea that best solves a problem is found.

To increase the likelihood of a successful process, one should include key stakeholders such as advisors, collaborators, partners, or even coaches. As Katherine Phillips shares in her article, "How Diversity Makes Us Smarter," introducing individuals with different disciplinary and cultural backgrounds into the conversation "encourages the search for novel information and perspectives, leading to better decision-making and problem-solving. Diversity can improve the bottom line of companies and lead to unfettered discoveries and breakthrough innovations."[17]

Incorporating the views of others in your process demonstrates a level of trust and an appreciation of their opinion, which cultivates a culture of mutual respect and collaboration. Jim Harter at Gallup, an analytics and advisory firm shared that "highly-engaged employees produce substantially better outcomes, are more likely to stay at their organization and experience less burn-out. In my experience, employees generally cannot reach that level unless they feel invested in their work, are given opportunities to develop their strengths, and understand how their role contributes to the company's overall success."[18]

When making critical decisions, it is important for leaders to cultivate a culture of collaboration by actively recruiting stakeholders to openly share and debate the ideas proposed. In doing so, you will foster an environment where participants trust and learn from one another, as well as serve to ensure everyone is working toward a common goal. Purposefully taking the opportunity to involve others in your decision-making process will serve you in establishing more meaningful relationships, building bridges of trust, and creating an invaluable leadership-development experience by empowering others to leverage their knowledge, experience, and relationships to achieve a desired objective.

Transparency

Effective decision-making needs to be a balance between the inputs and perspectives of the leader(s) and those of the group being led. Effective and appropriate decision-making strategies promote positive company culture and outcomes. The key to a successful balance includes creativity, practicality, and data-driven results to expand the overall efficacy of decision-making creativity in the workplace.

Collaborative leaders encourage their teams to actively, rather than passively, participate in the decision-making process. The reason for this is that those individuals who are most profoundly affected by a decision are usually more connected to the topic than an external "expert." It's for this reason that these types of leaders are mindful of their employees' perspectives, as their success hinges on their team's commitment to follow through on the resulting outcome. Conversely, an autocratic leader's process for making decisions doesn't allow for feedback and debate with colleagues and members of their team. In doing so, these types of leaders make decisions with the expectation that orders will be universally accepted, implemented, and without any questions.

While the latter scenario might expedite the decision-making process, it might also diminish their team's buy-in and potentially their long-term retention. Good decision-making requires leaders to trust their ability to effectively assess and make a decision, while simultaneously trusting their team's ability to generate and propose alternate ideas. Balancing both participating parties' creativity is a necessary foundation of a transparent and effective decision-making process. This balancing act creates a culture of collaboration, which is far more likely to produce consistently better decisions that result in positive outcomes, which in turn cultivates a higher level of employee satisfaction, as well as optimizes the decision-making process. This is how good group decisions are made.

When we work together, better choices can be made, and this might be crucial if the decision is an important one. Taking into consideration additional points of view by consulting with key stakeholders prior to making a decision will provide objective perspectives to help ensure success. Lastly, for public or potentially political decisions, taking the time to educate and inform stakeholders will help to ensure the ultimate decision is well received.

Involving Others

Is this my decision alone or are there others who should participate? Do I need to invite additional stakeholders to participate in the decision-making process? Do I need to develop consensus prior to making and communicating a decision? Particularly in the case of significant decisions, I find it essential to engage individuals who might be directly or indirectly responsible or accountable for areas or individuals impacted.

I am always amazed to observe decisions that appear to have an obvious choice or outcome, only to find there are stakeholders who have a completely different perspective and vehemently oppose the direction the "obvious" choice would take. It's with this perspective that we need to recognize that every individual will view a decision through his or her "lens." A lens that has been shaped by their personal experience, biases, training, etc.

Take for example, a toy manufacturer that is in the midst of its annual budgeting process. In alignment with their corporate growth strategy, executives are actively debating on whether to allocate additional budget to the redesign and expansion of their existing product line. A product line that historically focused on the outdoor and sports toy market segment, having consistently outperformed the company's annual sales projections; however the market segment is projected to experience its first market contraction in years.[19] Anticipating a potential shift in consumer purchasing habits, management has brought on a new sales leader to spearhead the smart toys market, which is projected to outperform virtually every other segment and one that is still highly fragmented, providing a potentially exceptional growth opportunity for the organization.

Having come from the software development industry, the new sales leader views investments in innovation as a no-brainer and a necessity to effectively compete. In her experience, consumers present an ever-constant demand for new functions and features, as their prior organization failed to adequately invest in innovation and therefore faced product obsolescence. Conversely, the CFO, a twenty-year veteran at the company, sees the market contraction as a small hiccup. Based on his experience and personal bias that the organization will confidently navigate these types of market fluctuations, he concludes that it is more important to focus on their core offering as a means to protect their existing position and protect their limited financial resources—their "war chest."

In this example, each executive might have valid reasons to support their position. However, it is clear that their positions and how they view this decision have been influenced by their experience and personal bias. While the sales leader's goal is to cultivate and grow a new product offering for the organization, it is the CFO's responsibility to maintain the company's financial health and ensure they have the necessary resources to compete and grow in subsequent years. It is for this reason that it is critical to involve others in your decisions so that you are able to come to a well-rounded decision that best supports the organization's goals, mission, and values.

Informed Stakeholders

While you might be empowered to make a decision, have you asked yourself what the politics and implications are? In many cases, these might not change your decision, but they may help to shape the method or approach used to communicate. Speaking for myself, but also more broadly, I've found that no one likes surprises or looking foolish. As a result, the success of your decisions often lies in your understanding of the audience and their associated behaviors. Making decisions in isolation is one of the quickest and most effective methods to achieve failure, despite doing everything else correctly. Human nature drives our interest to participate in the decision-making process, particularly if there are significant implications. When a key stakeholder's role is diminished or they don't have an opportunity to participate, they have a tendency to instantly become an adversary, or worse, become nefarious by trying to undermine the outcome of a decision.

Personal Aside

To be completely candid, at numerous points throughout my career, I wanted to be the hero and tackle problems by myself. I sought the glory of solving a crisis or making "*the big sale,*" as well as the credibility gained for having successfully resolved the issue or delivered the project on my own. This inclination was partially born from my own insecurities, as I never wanted to ask for help, or worse, felt I would burden someone else with my issue. Another factor was my misdirected career drive, as I believed that a critical component of my career success was an ability to resolve complex problems myself. I found out very quickly that working alone brings little credit, and heroes do not work alone.

Years after I'd begun my career on the institutional trading desks at Sempra Energy and Morgan Stanley, I transitioned into risk management consulting for one of the "Big 4" audit and consulting firms. For those unfamiliar with the term, the Big 4 refers to the largest accounting and consulting firms in the world: Deloitte, PwC, EY, and KPMG.

It was a seismic shift in cultures and how each type of organization made critical decisions. A shift that spanned styles of leadership, communication, collaboration, and virtually every other aspect of decision-making imaginable!

For my first Big 4 consulting project, we sold an organizational transformation engagement at a money management firm located in Santa Monica, California. As a visual learner, the catalyst for our sale was a process map I quickly pulled together following our initial meeting with the client. I had no intention of sharing it with the client, as I'd built it for my own purposes to help me visually walk through their processes and identify potential gaps.

In looking over my shoulder, the lead client services partner saw what I had drafted and asked me to immediately print out a copy.

Bumbling, I stuttered, stating that it wasn't ready for the client. Confident in the message it would carry, he brushed off my response and persistently presented it to our client's CFO. By demonstrating how we could quickly assess and identify organizational risks, he sold the first of what became a series of engagements with this client. I thought to myself, I made it! I had successfully moved cross-country and made the transition into consulting at one of the largest firms in the world. Drawing upon my interest in teaching, I was now in a role to help others by sharing the "vast knowledge" I had gained in my still budding career.

For our initial engagement, I was tasked with assessing and providing recommendations meant to optimize the bank's operational processes and their adoption of technology, with the explicit intent of increasing productivity and ensuring they were able to meet their regulatory obligations. As one of two members of our team who had previous experience working on a trading desk, I felt fairly confident in my knowledge and perspective. Almost immediately, I identified a critical issue with how they were reconciling their clients' trading accounts. This posed a significant risk to the organization and I believed it needed to be addressed immediately. Taking the same problem-solving approach I would have taken back at Morgan Stanley, I sought counsel from our firm's leading subject matter expert. I did this to confirm my observation and to receive help in developing a recommendation for how the client should resolve the identified issue.

With no ill intentions, I had just set off a firestorm for myself. First off, I made the decision to involve a partner outside of our client service team and did not first coordinate my communications through my director. While my actions might have been appropriate for a trading desk, within consulting there is an unwritten rule (at least for me at the time) that you are required to route such a request through the "chain of command" before taking action. At the time it seemed like bullshit to me. From my vantage point, it appeared as though the director wanted to take credit for my work without a sufficient understanding of the issue identified and the risks it created for our client. However, the director viewed the sequence of events as a complete usurpation of their power, position, and responsibility. Secondly, the partner who I had contacted subsequently reached out to our lead client service partner, offering to provide "assistance"—meaning they sought to insert themself into our team. While it may sound like consulting partners are collaborative, they are extremely territorial over their accounts and revenue streams. Although I was ultimately right in my observation and recommendation, my lack of understanding of firm politics wound up leaving a residual negative impression on the director, despite the fact we ended up winning additional work as a result of my efforts.

Why Collaboration is Important

Self-awareness and the ability to recognize your blind spots are critical aspects of what makes an effective leader and separates them from their peers. While you might think you know your blind spots, research suggests otherwise. In a survey conducted by psychologist Tasha Eurich, she found "amongst 467 working adults in the US, 95% of people think they're self-aware, but only 10% to 15% actually are." Meaning, the majority of people are prone to these types of shortcomings and what makes this so dangerous is that most don't know it. It's by establishing a culture of collaboration that we are able to mitigate the risks that might arise from single-minded decision-making. Further, Eurich noted, "99% of respondents across several industries reported working with at least one such person, and nearly half worked with at least four. Peers were the most frequent offenders (with 73% of respondents reporting at least one unaware peer), followed by direct reports (33%), bosses (32%), and clients (16%)."[20]

Adopting a culture of collaboration that intentionally seeks out pertinent information that invites the perspectives of key stakeholders, as well as involving your team in the decision-making process, will benefit your entire organization. By aligning with your peers on a specific goal or objective, freely sharing information, and fostering open (*and potentially contentious*) debates on the elements of a decision will serve to strengthen relationships amongst colleagues. Further, the quality of your decisions will improve, due to having the right mix of skills and expertise at the table. On top of this, you'll also have the right people in place who are prepared and ready to execute based on an agreed-upon action plan.

📝 Self-Study Questions:

- Have I taken the time to assess the impact of a decision, those who may have an influential opinion, will be responsible for carrying it out, or who will be impacted, and assess the appropriate level of socialization required?
- Are there additional stakeholders with a vested interest or who will be impacted that I should consult or collaborate with on a decision?
- Did I share with the key influencers the analysis performed, options available, and suggested recommendations, before requesting approval on a final decision?
- Does everyone who agrees with my decision "look" and "feel" like me, or have I taken into consideration a broader and diverse set of stakeholders?

PRINCIPLE 4:
RECOGNIZE COGNITIVE BIAS

Eliminating Mental Blinders Creates
More Productive Outcomes

"I think unconscious bias is one of the hardest things to get at."
— **RUTH BADER GINSBURG**

Do you have emotional ties that might affect your decision? Are you able to identify blinders that you or others might have that contribute to a sense of overconfidence in our personal or organizational capabilities, or place artificial limits on what can be accomplished as a result of establishing a symbolic anchor? Can you identify and redirect these pre-conclusions to help ensure the decisions at hand are objectively evaluated prior to making a final selection? Personal bias is a trap to which even the most experienced leaders fall victim from time to time. Your success lies in having the self-awareness to recognize situations where an inherent bias might be influencing the views of a pending decision. Acknowledging these biases and taking the appropriate actions will allow you to mitigate their potentially negative effects before having to make a final decision. As a result, you are far more likely to achieve the desired outcome.

Based on our beliefs, upbringing, and experience, we all have inherent biases. The most common among these biases are overconfidence, confirmation, anchoring, and the false consensus effect. Sometimes these biases are obvious, but in other cases, these biases are so subtle that they might be difficult to notice in ourselves and even in others.

This was a lesson I learned from my father early in life. Ironic as it might sound, our closest personal connection were conversations about his toils from having built a wholesale printing equipment and supplies company that spanned much of New York State, as well as several adjacent states. The son of an immigrant and armed with only a high school diploma, my father often felt inferior to his competition, a lifelong insecurity that drove him to become a voracious reader, mindful observer, and calculated risk-taker. It was during one particular exchange that he boldly predicted the downfall of Kodak's photographic film business line. As I recall, he described their management as misinformed and cocky. A preposterous statement at the time as their founder, George Eastman, had invented the roll film used in handheld cameras and maintained an industry-leading position through the 1990s, controlling 80% of the US market alone.[21] Prior to the advent of digital cameras and Apple's integration of digital cameras within the smartphone, handheld cameras were the mainstream solution for photography and one that was extremely profitable.

Observing the aggressive marketing and pricing tactics taken by their main competitor Fujifilm, he'd concluded that Kodak failed to respond in a timely fashion and, therefore, its photographic film business line was at risk. Kodak's headquarters were and still are located in Rochester, New York, which, coincidentally, is the city where my father launched his career and still did a tremendous amount of business. He'd recognized that Fujifilm purposely avoided selling its products in the region, which contributed to a misinformed confirmation mindset for Kodak's executives about their competition. Further, they held onto overconfident projections of future sales growth based on a notably long, strong, and resilient sales history. Having spent his entire career selling printing equipment and supplies he knew all too well that consumers held no loyalty, especially if there was a cheaper substitute that delivered the same level of quality.

With this as a given, what can you do to mitigate potentially negative presumptions in your decision-making process? To mitigate the risk of personal bias, we need to learn how to remain open-minded, allowing ourselves to challenge our assumptions. This should be demonstrated in a manner that promotes creative and open-minded thinking, able to overcome potentially negative preconceptions. Successful leaders seek to establish an environment where it is acceptable and encouraged to challenge the status quo, ask hard questions, or suggest creative out-of-the-box solutions.

Let's break down a few of the more common cognitive biases and address how they might influence your thoughts, feelings, and behavior.

The Overconfidence Bias

While virtually everyone mistakenly falls for the overconfidence bias at some point or another, I find it affects a disproportionately larger percentage of athletes and entrepreneurs. Having personally succeeded and failed at each of these, I have a particularly keen understanding of its main drivers. It's a personal belief that you are better equipped and possess more knowledge than those before you or those you will be competing against. Applying this to business, the overconfidence bias manifests itself in many ways including overestimating our ability to achieve a particular outcome, complete a project within a given deadline, or manage to operate within a stated budget.

The overconfidence bias, also known as the overconfidence effect, often causes people to erroneously inflate their skills and knowledge.

People who suffer from overconfidence bias often lack an objective view of their abilities.

Examples of this include:

- Expecting to replicate prior success without taking into consideration new information or factors available.
- Believing in your ability to succeed, despite an overabundance of information supporting the contrary.
- Tendency to take credit for one's success and blame others for their failures.

Overconfidence bias is a personal trait that is frequently instilled and shaped by external influences, such as our family, friends, and beliefs considered to be social norms. Individualistic cultures, like that of the United States, often defer and celebrate individuals who demonstrate the brazen confidence exemplified by the country's pioneers and cowboys. If not held in check, overconfidence can and will become problematic. Often those exuding the greatest amount of confidence have the least amount of knowledge or ability to back it up. And due to their confidence, they are likely the last people to invest the time and energy necessary to become successful.

The Confirmation Bias

When prompted with a politically charged decision, do you seek input from a variety of perspectives or primarily those who agree with your position? Sources range from colleagues, vendors, news outlets, and other information channels such as Facebook. All too often, I have found that leaders naturally seek out sources that agree with their position and not ones from a contradictory or objective perspective.

Confirmation bias is the propensity to seek out individuals and information sources that serve only to reconfirm and validate our existing beliefs and conclusions. As a result, we frequently favor and are more likely to trust those sources who share similar points of view and conclusions we already believe or have made a decision on.

Examples of this include:
- Selectively choosing to discuss your views with individuals who you know agree on a particular issue.
- Actively participating in the practice of writing or forwarding emails composed of selective facts and stories that support your position.
- Actively ignoring opposing positions and their underlying reasoning, opinions, and supporting facts.

There are a few reasons why this happens. The predominant factor I have found is our ego and an inherent tendency to want to be right, even when presented with well-minded reasoning and clear facts on the contrary. Other factors include our preference to expedite the decision-making process and minimize the resources required to assess and make a conclusion.

In addition, I have found that we are predisposed to filter out the information we hear that supports an opposing view. Instead, we unconsciously choose to listen to points of view that support our position. Despite having a career that's spanned over two decades, I am always surprised to find executives who after leaving a meeting walk away with completely different interpretations of the information that was presented and the decisions that were made. The problem with this is that it can lead to tunnel vision, by having considered a selective portion of the information and feedback provided by others, which might result in a poor decision with a counterproductive outcome.

The Anchoring Bias

Particularly during pricing negotiations but applicable to all types of decision-making scenarios, a highly effective negotiation technique used to convince other parties—as well as yourself—of the accuracy of a decision is to establish an initial data point for all parties to consider. An anchor.

The anchoring bias is the propensity to ground our perspective based on the first data point we are presented with. Whether it's derived from an article we read or a business negotiation tactic, it serves to influence our thinking and establish expectations or limitations about a particular topic. As a result, the anchoring bias frequently clouds our judgment and ability to objectively assess and consider the options available before making a final conclusion.

Examples of this include:

- During pricing negotiations, volunteering the first number in an effort to establish an arbitrary floor or ceiling on the value of a product or service, with the goal of influencing the views of others.
- During an emergency room visit, the results of a patient's initial triage assessment influence subsequent decisions, despite the onset of new symptoms or additional information provided by new data sources.
- An art gallery promoting a particular artist's work uses previous sales prices of successful pieces sold by the artist to substantiate the initial offering price.

The anchoring bias can be dangerous and have particularly negative implications for individuals who are uninformed or lack the confidence to stand by their views and analysis, a bias that frequently infiltrates our thinking and the decisions we make on a daily basis. It's when we assume the information we are presented with was based on facts, where, in many instances, they are based on strategies meant to purposely influence your thinking and, therefore, your decisions.

The False Consensus Effect

In the midst of delivering a particularly high-profile postmortem report, I am often asked to attend, present our findings, participate in a client's executive deliberations, and ultimately assist with the development of a remediation plan. It's in those tense times that I have often found executive stakeholders might easily agree with the initial conclusion and the action plan developed, only to subsequently reverse their position unbeknownst to other stakeholders. This is not limited to high-stress situations, but applicable to virtually every type of decision.

The false consensus effect is the propensity to believe others agree and are aligned with your position and point of view. Often accompanying a critical or politically charged decision, we tend to overestimate the amount of support we have garnered and the level of intent and integrity others have in carrying through on their commitments.

Why is this?

There are a wide variety of reasons this occurs, such as the shifting needs of an organization, competing priorities requiring you to pull back on allocated resources, or simply an overextended executive. Each of these scenarios is explainable and will likely get flagged as you actively measure progress toward your intended objective. It will also alert you to the existence and influence of ever-present politics and personal ambitions, which can derail your decision. As unfortunate as it may sound, I have witnessed firsthand executives who agreeably supported a decision made during group discussion, only to find out in a subsequent debrief session that they have no intention of following through on their commitment. It's in these scenarios that you need to rely on the role of your decision champion to hold key stakeholders accountable for their support and commitments.

Examples of this include:

- Myopic views on what is right and overestimating the number of people who share the same beliefs and conclusion.
- Basing a decision on a handful of conversations with similarly minded executives, believing the discussions represented a majority opinion.
- Optimistic views on the integrity of others and their commitments to carry through on activities they never intended to perform or support.

The false consensus effect stems from several key influences we often leverage when making decisions. Familiarity, in that we typically associate and surround ourselves with like-minded people, particularly our family and friends. As a result, we have an inherent propensity to believe the same is true with our colleagues. A dangerous and misinformed personal view that our way of thinking and conclusions are the predominant view in a business setting.

Second, is our ego. Believing that others think, act, and have similar values is good for our self-esteem. Similar to the aforementioned friends and family example, believing others agree and align with our views allows us to feel normal and helps to instill personal confidence, particularly when comparing yourself to those with an opposing view. This is a dangerous position, as we often overvalue our own opinions, and, therefore, overlook how we will be viewed and the potentially negative implications our decisions will have on others.

Let's look at some additional examples of common biases.

The Misinformation Effect

The misinformation effect is a propensity that causes us to unconsciously alter our memories based on information, stories, or events that are shared or occur after the event. As adults, we often attempt to recall events that occurred during our childhood, only to find out that our crystal-clear memory was created as a result of an embellished story shared years later. Surprisingly, researchers have found that our memories are susceptible to even very subtle influences, such as questions asked after the fact or listening to the description of events as told by independent observers.

Examples of this include:
- A lawyer pressing a witness to answer questions about an event, causing the witness to make assumptions on what occurred or alter their memory of what happened.
- Watching a documentary, listening to a podcast, or reading a news article on a given subject can alter how someone recalls an event.
- Listening to the views and opinions about an event from someone who holds different values or perspectives can shape how we view and remember how an event started or unfolded.

While we often chalk up the misinformation effect as having subtle, if not inconsequential effects on our memories, it's those recollections that we also categorize as our experience. A powerful asset we value and often draw upon to make better and more well-informed future decisions. Should our memories be clouded, if not altered by the misinformation effect, it's easy to see how this can have detrimental and compounding impacts on our decisions. You might not only be making the wrong decision, but might also find yourself blinded with overconfidence and, therefore, less apt to take feedback from others.

The Actor-Observer Bias

The actor-observer bias is the propensity to attribute the outcomes of an action, activity, or decision differently should you be the actor or the observer. When we are the actor, we have full knowledge of our own thoughts and the external influences or circumstances that might have impacted the outcome. Particularly, for those that failed or led to a negative result, we allow ourselves to absolve and deflect the reasoning to external factors beyond our control.

All the while, when we are the observer there is a propensity to conclude the reasoning for a failed or negative outcome sits solely on the responsible individual or organization. Depending on the severity, we often call into question their knowledge, competency, values, or lack of execution. In the case of the actor-observer bias, we overlook external influences, as well as countless other inputs and variables that might have impacted their decision and the resulting outcome.

In the case of an actor-observer bias, I cannot overstate the impact your role—whether as actor or observer—plays in influencing your perspective on a decision and the resulting outcome. The critical difference between the two roles is that as the actor, we have access to our thoughts, influences, behaviors, and circumstances related to a situation. As observers, we only have access to information collected from what we have witnessed firsthand and presume to understand what the person or organization was thinking, their influences, behaviors, and preceding events that might have impacted their actions.

Examples of this include:
- Having prepared for an upcoming deposition, an "actor" failed to deliver a convincing explanation as a result of exhaustion due to jet lag. Conversely, an observer at the same deposition might conclude the interviewee failed to substantiate their case due to lack of preparation, or that they were at fault and are attempting to deflect culpability.
- Two students having a quiet conversation are perceived by an observing teacher as disruptive and disciplined accordingly. As the actors, one student had missed several days of school due to illness and the second was sympathetic and simply trying to help by explaining what the other missed.

The critical issue with the actor-observer bias is that it frequently leads us to develop drastically different opinions and conclusions about an individual, event, or decision. Blaming an individual for a failed decision, without taking into consideration the external variables, provides a narrow view of the situation itself. This often creates a lasting misunderstanding amongst involved stakeholders that can contribute to long-term tension amongst colleagues.

The Self-Serving Bias

How often do we find someone patting themselves on the back for their successes and then finding scapegoats to blame for when they fail to achieve a desired goal? The self-serving bias is a propensity for stakeholders to take credit for their successes but lay the blame for failures on external factors. Self-serving leaders tend to view productive outcomes as an expected result of their strong decision-making process. Yet, when an outcome doesn't achieve a desired goal, they immediately seek to identify the nefarious actor or unanticipated complication for their failure.

Examples of this include:
- Stakeholders who tout an infallible ability to recall past events and proceed to challenge and undermine others who present a different recollection.
- An individual related to a hiring manager concludes they were hired based on their intellect and experience, and dispersing thoughts that it was due to nepotism.

Self-serving bias is a potentially lethal mindset that can destroy careers, and is shaped by our upbringing, education, and values, as well as influenced by our age, title, and previous experiences. Leaders who were able to climb the corporate ladder at the expense of others are more likely to take credit for their successes and pin failures on outside forces. In the short term, a self-serving bias often cultivates a false sense of personal confidence and serves to support a distorted view of ourselves, our abilities, and our limitations.

Conclusion

Cognitive bias is both an asset and a liability to our decision-making process. They are more common than we give them credit for and the aforementioned list is only a sampling of the many biases that can influence our thinking. They are thought processes created as a result of our upbringing and prior experiences, meant to assist with expediting the time and mind space required to make a decision. However, if we are not mindful of the influence biases can have on our thinking, especially at the speed and volume we as humans are required to make decisions today, they have the potential of undermining our ability to make an objective and well-informed conclusion.

Mind you, often more than just one bias can be at play at any time, shaping our thoughts about a particular decision and, therefore, unconsciously swaying our perspective and conclusions. Collectively, these biases can make it exponentially more difficult to discern which ones are influencing our decisions. To mitigate the impact of biases on our decision-making, effective leaders cultivate collaborative cultures that support an open discourse on critical decisions, even encouraging stakeholders to purposely question the reasoning used to support a contributor's position and potentially biased motivations related to decisions that more often produce better outcomes that are aligned with our objectives.

It is inevitable that cognitive bias can and will influence our thinking, as we simply don't have the time to filter and evaluate every thought and decision for the presence of bias. Mindfully reminding ourselves to assess the presence and influence biases have on our thinking, as well as remaining open and receptive to others' questions and pushback will help us shape and make increasingly more well-informed decisions.

📝 Self-Study Questions:

- Have I dismissed others' questions and opinions for the sake of my preconceived ideas and potentially hardwired biases?
- Have I sufficiently evaluated the experiences and perspectives of others and how they came to a different conclusion when given the same information?
- Am I jumping to a conclusion based on a previous event or experience, without taking the time to effectively understand new information and influences available to me?
- Have I cultivated a culture that encourages team members to challenge ideas in a positive and collaborative manner, with the goal of achieving greater results or outcomes?

PRINCIPLE 5:
ESTABLISH A CHAMPION

Visionary Leaders Able to Provide Credibility and **Influence Others**

"The most difficult thing is the decision to act, the rest is merely tenacity."
—AMELIA EARHART

Have you ever met someone who appeared to always make the right decision and achieve their desired goals, if not outperform them? Do they have some innate business sense or is it something else? That *je ne sais quoi* quality of a champion is the ability to effectively manage relationships and the political landscape, sensing where there will be pushback or roadblocks, and then crafting amicable solutions meeting the needs of all vested parties. And while these individuals likely have a finely tuned executive skill set to guide their decisions, it's those who employ the role of a champion in their decision-making process who are far more likely to succeed and accomplish their goals.

Highly effective champions are often influential senior executives, who recognize the importance of crucial management decisions, particularly when they are tied to large, complex, or politically charged organizational initiatives. Unless this is a role you plan to fulfill, I suggest recruiting a champion early in your decision-making process. An informed champion who has been provided the opportunity to make meaningful contributions to the decision-making process is far more likely to take ownership of achieving the desired outcome. They will, therefore, be a more credible supporter, able to educate and advocate the benefits of a decision and how it supports a well-defined objective.

Attributes of a highly effective champion:
- A committed supporter of a decision and the desired outcome.
- A persuasive communicator and effective negotiator.
- An inspirational and motivating leader.
- Knowledgeable, if not an expert, on the given subject.
- Possesses the authority to engage influential executives and key stakeholders.

Driving Accountability

Core qualities of an effective champion are their ability to cultivate stakeholder awareness and support, as well as nurture a culture of accountability to increase the likelihood of a positive outcome. This is particularly true for complex organizations, where it often boils down to relationship management; either selling or influencing critical stakeholders on the benefits of a decision, and then following through to monitor progress and ensure critical stakeholders keep their commitments. A decision made by an executive or management committee does not guarantee follow-through or ongoing support. As I shared earlier, I have observed more than enough situations where an individual or committee member agreed to a decision, and then subsequently privately shared with me that they never intended to support the decision and its underlying project or activity.

It's by defining your desired objectives in simple terms and establishing the critical path required to achieve your goals that enable champions to effectively monitor the business and political landscape, as well as hold stakeholders accountable. As I am sure you are all too familiar with, the ability to anticipate and identify potential risks and roadblocks is essential to avoiding threats that might have impeded or derailed an otherwise successful decision. Examples of this include engaging and educating uninformed or dissenting stakeholders, escalating resource requests, or simply contributing their insights and moral support.

This reminds me of a particularly effective champion, who I had the fortune to collaborate with and learned much about the power of persuasion. At the time, he was the chief executive officer for a large hospital and played a pivotal role in launching a new strategic joint venture with their contracted health insurers and referring independent physician practices. The plan proposed asked participating organizations to collaboratively share patient information, to improve the coordination and delivery of their patient's health care.

It goes without saying that there is an inherent level of distrust within the health care industry.

A simplified description of their roles and responsibilities:

- Health insurers are financially responsible for their members, seeking to provide the highest level of care for the lowest contracted rates.
- Hospitals invest in and manage facilities able to deliver the highest-quality medical care available as a means of attracting patient referrals and negotiating profitable reimbursement rates with health insurers.

Independent physicians are responsible for their patient's health, and are therefore seeking to partner with hospitals able to provide the requisite facilities and services, and who have an established contract with their patient's health insurance provider.

Empathy and Influencing Others

Had it not been for this leader's ability to proactively establish influential relationships and lay the groundwork for a mutually beneficial joint venture, this aspirational endeavor would have been dead on inception. By developing relationships with key leaders from each organization and listening to the fears and concerns of the divided parties, he was able to effectively gain consensus amongst critical and resistant stakeholders. By taking the time to understand the needs of each party, he led the collaborative design of a joint venture that would both benefit and protect each stakeholder's interests.

As the default leader of this new entity, he skillfully gleaned the necessary information from his interactions to refine our strategic plan and also provide his personal assurance to every stakeholder that it was in their best interest to participate. He emphasized that the alternative would result in a far worse outcome, which was to either succumb to an acquisition by a larger entity or a continual decline in market share and shrinking profit margins.

By keeping stakeholders focused on the new entity's objectives, he was able to navigate many of the obstacles and constraints raised throughout the initial stages of the joint venture. In simple terms, the new entity's goals were to reduce the cost of patient care for insurers, improve the quality of care delivered to the patients, and increase the financial health of both the hospital and their referring independent physician practices. An incredible step in the delivery of coordinated health care, which would have been unimaginable a decade earlier.

Maintaining Momentum

As I shared with you before, decision-making is not just something that occurs at a point in time, but rather is a process—one that will frequently shift and evolve as a result of changes in the organization's priorities, personnel, and a multitude of other factors. A champion is not only a decision advocate but one who actively monitors the business and political landscape, anticipating threats and roadblocks that could impede or derail a critical decision or project. Highly effective champions are adept at managing these inevitable events, recognizing that it is a necessary function of their role. In many scenarios, the success of a decision lies in the follow-through and not the actual decision itself. After a decision has been finalized, one of the critical factors in your success will be the ability to identify what additional activities are required to ensure sustained progress and a successful outcome.

Having observed clients who failed to accomplish their goals, I found that maintaining momentum is one of the most critical aspects in achieving a successful outcome for your decision. Similar to the mindset required to complete a marathon, a decision's champion maintains the stakeholder's focus and interest on a desired outcome to successfully achieve the objectives necessary to cross the proverbial finish line.

Applicable to a single decision, as well as complex programs consisting of thousands of small decisions, a lack of focus will frequently undermine an organization and its leaders' ability to achieve their goals—an often overlooked skill set, and yet the evidence of its impact is staggering. According to Gartner, more than 75 percent of enterprise resource planning (ERP) system implementations fail to achieve their desired objectives.[22] Meanwhile, global consultancy McKinsey estimates that more than 70 percent of all digital transformations fail to accomplish their goals.[23]

Establishing Consensus and Support

As you would expect, one of the important roles of a champion is to ensure all critical and influential stakeholders associated with a given decision are on board—particularly for instances where their decisions might have a potentially broad or significant impact on an organization's personnel, departments, and customers. Recognizing that some stakeholders might not see the value of a decision or the resulting project, they might choose to take a dissenting position and, therefore, withhold their support and resources necessary to achieve your desired outcome.

A champion helps to convey the strategic vision and value of a decision, particularly those that are critical to an organization's ability to achieve its mission and goals. They help in educating senior executive stakeholders on the background, benefits, and necessity for a given decision and the resulting activities, which might include actions such as a purchase acquisition, alterations to the structure and composition of an organization's workforce, or approval to move forward with a new system implementation.

Motivating Others

Often in challenging situations, the views of key stakeholders might drift and the enthusiasm of individuals responsible for carrying out the resulting activities stemming from a decision simply wanes. It's for this reason that a champion must recognize these types of changes and the obstacles each present, and when necessary, take on the role of an inspirational leader and promoter.

Using the attributes of the North Star they had carefully defined, a champion actively promotes the benefits of the path chosen and why a particular decision serves to provide the greatest benefit and outcome. At times, they might choose to directly engage an individual or team, seeking to understand their concerns and provide them with personal reassurances on the value and necessity of the work they're performing and praising them for the value they have contributed toward a desired outcome.

Eliminating Obstacles

An often-overlooked component of a champion's role is the use of their authority to handle company politics. Often, we find ourselves faced with an obstacle that is related to personal differences or issues between organization personnel. Due to their senior standing, a champion can help manage organizational politics to keep key stakeholders focused on the intended objective.

When a decision comes up against an issue, such as a resource limitation impacting productivity, budgets, or delivery schedules, the champion must have the authority to negotiate with the executive group to obtain the resources necessary to successfully stay on track. If the decision at hand is part of a larger program or corporate initiative, they can also work with their teams and individual contributors to assess potential impediments or competing priorities, and the implications of a decision based on the organization's priorities and values. A champion is able to assist their teams in navigating these types of issues and ultimately make a higher-quality decision, as well as coach the individual contributors on how to evaluate their options and select the one that best aligns with their objective. This is a form of mentoring that serves to develop decisive leaders, by instilling the knowledge and tools required to make better choices that result in consistently more successful and productive outcomes.

Ensuring Success

It's almost inevitable that decisions, particularly those that are high profile or might have a broad impact on an organization, will encounter obstacles along the way—often driven by an individual's fear of the unknown, resistance to change, or resource limitations stemming from a competing priority. It's an important role of a champion to get the necessary buy-in from key and influential stakeholders early and in a timely manner. The alternative introduces unnecessary risks to your desired outcome. Creating an opportunity for objectors, obstacles, and alternate options to become cemented impediments to accomplishing your goals. I have found that it's human nature for executive stakeholders to go on the defensive if they feel that they weren't brought into the decision-making process early enough, and, therefore, likely to withhold their support and vote against it.

Gaining stakeholder buy-in requires a champion—one who is able to clearly convey a vision, articulate the benefits of a decision, quell concerns and objections, and be willing to leverage their political capital to ensure everyone stays aligned with the desired outcome. Whether that's pushing to expedite an approval, navigating a politically charged discussion, or avoiding foreseeable impediments altogether, that person becomes the "face" of the decision to ensure its success.

Even if a decision was your idea, you might not necessarily be the optimal champion or conversely, you might see it as an opportunity to empower others to gain the experience of being one. If there's a stakeholder with sufficient authority who believes as wholeheartedly as you do in a particular goal and has relevant expertise for getting stakeholder buy-in, such as experience in change management or exceptionally persuasive communication skills, they might be well-suited for the task. However, in a small department or organization, you might not have that luxury, and you'll need to wear the "champion" hat yourself.

📝 Self-Study Questions:

- Who is the optimal individual to champion a decision and have they been incorporated sufficiently to support a successful outcome?
- What potential roadblocks exist that might negatively impact the outcome of a decision, such as competing timelines, budgets, priorities, or politics?
- Have I identified and empowered the key supporters required for a successful outcome?
- Have I identified potential detractors or advocates of the status quo who might seek to undermine the desired outcome?

PRINCIPLE 6:

MANAGE FALLOUT

Integrity and Legacy Start with
**Awareness, Empathy, and
Helping Others**

"Do not base your decisions on the advice of those who will not have to deal with the results."
—ANONYMOUS

Have you ever contemplated the impact of a decision before you made it, particularly assessing how it would affect those who might be negatively impacted? Of course, you have.

I learned at an early age that even something as simple as offering a smile or holding a door open for someone can brighten their day. Now imagine you are responsible for a business, a team, or even just one external consultant. What kind of impact do you suppose equivalent types of gestures would have on your business, employees, and extended third-party resources? What are the notable impacts or repercussions resulting from your decisions or indecisions? Even good decisions can have negative impacts on individuals and organizations. Taking the opportunity to engage and educate those impacted is a trait of an empathetic leader and, as a byproduct, may bear unexpected fruit.

Legacy, and the potential to influence future decisions, are often hinged on the ability to manage the fallout from our decisions. As part of this principle, we need to take a careful look at the negative effect we might have on an impacted stakeholder. As leaders, we need to act with integrity, own up to our decisions, and manage the fallout of our actions. We need to step in and help shepherd the communication and implementation of changes required or the result of external forces. This includes our need to act with empathy and seek to understand the impact of our decisions and, where appropriate, assist in the development of a complementary response workstream. As part of this stage, you should seek to understand any negative fallout from a decision and develop a response communication that educates those affected on why it was necessary, so as to ensure they continue to be supporters and contribute to an effective workforce.

Anticipating Fallout

Pushing further on this hot button, if given the opportunity to get in front of a decision and help to proactively engage those who had been or would be negatively impacted, would you? In my opinion, this is one of the most defining characteristics of a highly effective leader and a direct reflection of their integrity, as well as a mark of strong personal character. Whether it's a direct and empathetic conversation, a consolation email offering your support, or some other way of providing a meaningful touchpoint, these actions often have a profound effect on those affected, as well as your reputation and legacy. The alternative, essentially a lack of action, often contributes to lasting disdain and animosity for a leader and maybe the entire organization, which I have observed firsthand the results of which negatively impacted future sales, partnerships, and personal relationships.

Why is this? I would like to think positively and believe that it's not indifference or a lack of caring, but that leaders might not have the necessary skills to effectively and proactively manage the fallout. However, I have often found leaders justify the impact of a particular decision as a "business necessity," and that the casualties resulting from it were justified, therefore, allowing them to freely move forward while leaving those affected reeling.

Misjudging Your Impact on Others

It is tempting to ignore or underestimate the damage your decision will have upon those affected. While this might make you feel better about your decision, it usually adds insult to the person on the receiving end. For example, in the case of having to relocate a long-standing employee due to an organizational decision, it is important to recognize the sacrifice the individual will have to make, while not minimizing it by stating it will be a great opportunity for them and their family. While it might be easier for you to justify the decision to the employee, you are completely overlooking their personal needs for the sake of the business.

Regardless of what the decision is that you have to make, such as voting down a project, laying off an employee, or canceling a vendor contract, you still have the opportunity to positively influence the fallout and maintain what likely could have been a lost relationship. Many years ago, I read Daniel Goleman's book, *Emotional Intelligence: Why It Can Matter More Than IQ*,[24] which helped to shape how I view myself, my relationships, and most importantly, how I approach difficult decisions.

As human beings, it is virtually impossible to separate emotion from our decisions. We can choose to ignore or disregard it, but I truly believe it's a core component of our consciousness. Therefore, I found Goleman's illustration of the value and application of empathy and social skills to be highly effective in assessing and responding to the fallout of our decisions.

Empathy

An empathetic leader is one who takes a genuine interest in the well-being of others, their personal needs, the challenges they are confronted with, and most importantly their feelings. This not only applies to members of their team, but as well as their colleagues and those they have the ability to positively affect. They are ones who frequently seek to understand another's perspective, situation, and needs; and have the ability to put themselves in someone else's shoes. A critical skill of successful leaders is the ability to cultivate compassionate, collaborative, and supportive cultures to achieve an individual's and organization's objectives. And yet, I have found empathy remains an often overlooked leadership skill, particularly given the constant pressures today's workforce faces on a daily basis to meet performance goals and organizational growth objectives.

For example, a chief accounting officer (CAO) decides to implement a new accounting software platform, subsequently informing employees of the forthcoming change, and that additional updates to the team's structure and composition are still being worked out. This was a loyal team, many of whom had been in their roles for more than ten years.

Feeding off the company's rumor mill, vague hints of expected changes to the team's structure and requisite skills for key roles have invoked a new pessimistic culture, eroding employee morale, and increasing the likelihood that valuable team members will leave. Each presents a critical risk for the CAO, due to the accompanying loss of knowledge, relationships, and loyalty.

In this scenario, the CAO might want to consider implementing a different management style, one that captures the concerns of their team by engaging in direct communication about why change is necessary, what opportunities it will create, and providing an honest vision of what the employees' future roles will look like. As a result, the employees will feel valued and have greater confidence in their future and career, which in turn will increase their loyalty.

Social Skills

Effective leaders are often great communicators, confidently able to navigate the challenges we often face on a daily basis, as well as managing organizational change and resolving conflicts diplomatically and not sitting back while others do the work. They also use styles of communication that are clear, direct, and personal, and are open to feedback and flexible to adjust their messaging as necessary.

For example, the same CAO recognizes that as a result of an accounting platform's implementation and efficiencies gained, there is a high likelihood of a forthcoming change to their department's structure and potentially will no longer require several members of their existing team.

In this scenario, the CAO might want to sit down with each employee to explain why the implementation is a necessary improvement for the organization. Examples of this are commending an employee on the value they contributed toward the company's success, instilling confidence in their capabilities, and ability to successfully identify and adapt to a new role. It might also include offering assistance to either help them look for a new role within the department or offering to be a reference should they choose to leave. As a result, the CAO is far more likely to sustain a positive relationship with the employee and maintain their loyalty to the company.

An alternative approach, which I have also observed firsthand, is an executive leader delegating the communication of a pending layoff to a leader with no direct responsibility for the employee or an HR representative hired solely to execute a series of layoffs. As a result of this non-personalized approach and lack of personal integrity, the morale of the employee, their team, and the related department are essentially decimated. Due to the severity of this approach, it often creates a lasting feeling of animosity toward the company and its leaders.

While the benefits of both *empathy* and *social skills* appear simple and obvious, I have often witnessed leaders bypass these critical steps and leave those impacted in the wake to pick up the pieces.

Winners versus Losers

It's also easy to view a decision as picking the winners or losers, and then disparaging the "loser" as a way to support your decision. Imagine a scenario in which you're a regional president for a safety products manufacturer and due to a recent change in safety regulations, your sales have quadrupled. However, instead of celebrating, you're panic-stricken. Your manufacturing plants were already near capacity, as well as suffering from a strained supply chain for critical materials.

As your distribution team begins to assess the avalanche of incoming orders, your fears are quickly confirmed. Recognizing the broad implications the decision on which orders to fulfill, delay, or simply turn away is escalated to executive management. Not an easy decision, as essentially you will need to decide what customers will be the winners, as you fulfill their orders, and those whose orders you won't—the losers. This is a troubling scenario we have seen in recent years and one that fosters frustration with your customers, anger amongst your sales representatives, and exhaustion for an overburdened workforce.

In situations where a leader is asked to make these types of critical and unsavory decisions, it's not unusual to find the criteria used lacking objectivity while appearing justifiable. Whether favoritism for a sales representative or disdain for a particular customer, it's these types of knee-jerk conclusions that allow individuals to find solace in their decisions. While it might make it easier to stomach the harm caused, recognize it might have compromised the values of an individual and likely the organization's as well.

I will tell you from experience that this is a toxic approach. Instead, I recommend developing objective decision criteria that align with your mission, strategy, and values. When addressing those stakeholders who will bear the brunt of your decisions, I recommend taking an honest and transparent approach. When delivering an unsavory decision that results in unwanted harm, it's important to share the process and criteria used in making your conclusions.

Whether part of a formal communication plan or an executive's speaking point, it's crucial your message highlights that you acted with clear intent, which will help to mitigate and minimize the damage caused, as well as with recognizing the sacrifices made by those most affected by your decision.

Attributes of an Empathetic Leader:

- **Act with Clear Intent:** In the most genuine manner, clearly convey the reasoning and intention behind a forthcoming decision, particularly if it creates disruption, negatively impacts, or asks more of an individual, team, or organization.

- **Mitigate the Impact:** By anticipating the pending negative fallout from a decision, proactively seek opportunities to minimize the downside, and, where possible, provide opportunities that are ultimately more favorable for those affected. For the example given, consider how to compensate salespeople who will lose their commissions from the sales you were required to delay or cancel. An option might be to allow those orders to count toward the current period's bonus.

- **Demonstrate Compassion:** When presented with a decision that creates uncertainty for an individual, they often make the situation worse by jumping to conclusions as a result of obsessively imagining the worst outcome they will need to face. Anticipating these scenarios, proactively acknowledge the fears and concerns of those who might be affected, and reconfirm your commitment to support them through whatever transition they might be required to make.

- **Acknowledge Sacrifice:** Often our decisions require an individual, department, or organization to make unexpected sacrifices that impact their personal and professional lives. In these scenarios, an empathetic leader acknowledges their value and the contributions they have made. In addition, they share that a thoughtful approach was taken in assessing the potentially negative implications of a decision, before coming to a final conclusion. For the example given, acknowledge the challenging conversations your salespersons will need to have with disgruntled customers or the overtime you ask a production team to contribute until you are able to satisfy the increased demands.

The Value of Compassion

Why is empathy so important? In short, you never know how your decision-making process will ultimately impact an individual or organization. It is in these vulnerable times that you can have the most lasting impression on someone. Learning how to apply these techniques in your decision-making process will provide a lasting impact on those affected and on the outcomes of your most difficult choices. I truly have lived and breathed this philosophy. So much so that when someone was not empathetic or willing to seek to understand how a decision might impact a person or organization, I admittedly lost respect for them as a peer and an employee.

Personal Aside

The first company I started was a boutique firm specializing in health care regulatory and compliance consulting projects. Frequently our clients were executives in dire situations, driven by mandates handed down from their board of directors. In full transparency, the catalyst for launching my new company was based on personal necessity rather than bravado. It was February 2001, the peak of the worst global recession we have seen since the Great Depression. I had just been laid off and my wife was six months pregnant with our first daughter. With virtually no job prospects in my industry, one recruiter told me to expect a 50 percent reduction in salary. Unemployment or a significant reduction in compensation were not tenable outcomes that would meet my family's financial needs.

Admittedly, I was daunted by the idea of marketing a new service offering during a time period when most organizations were slashing budgets and laying off large segments of their workforce. Rather than chasing new prospects, I focused on clients with whom I had a previous working relationship and fostered strong relationships with their executive leaders. As fortune would have it, my first call was to a multibillion-dollar health care system for whom I had performed countless audits and assessments that frequently identified critical risks within the information technology (IT) organization's operations. Coincidentally, their board of directors had just delivered a directive for their chief information officer (CIO) to resolve a multitude of known and well-documented information security issues. Virtually every one of these issues had been identified and reported by teams who I had managed prior to being laid off.

Providing some contextual background, as was typical for not-for-profit health care systems at the time, information security was not a priority. Information security solutions were expensive and often not-for-profit health care systems ran at an operating loss. As demonstrated by their budgets, management's priorities were generally focused on investments to improve their delivery of patient care or increase their revenues. Information security did not fit into either of these categories.

Given their lack of funding, you can imagine their information security program was weak, and our historical assessment reports placed a spotlight directly on the most underserved areas. During my previous tenure auditing this client's IT operations, I developed a strong relationship with their CISO. Often, I found myself having lengthy conversations with him, discussing the results of our findings, why they were in each predicament, and how best to phrase our recommendations so that they could obtain the necessary resources required to address their needs. I approached each conversation with empathy, as I found him to be a particularly genuine person and an exceptional leader who understood the needs of the organization, and yet was often denied the resources required to address the gaps we had identified.

It was during one of these discussions that I recall the CISO bluntly asking me if I could help provide explicit direction on what changes were required and how to implement them; essentially I was being asked to design the solution. Unfortunately, I was responsible for overseeing their risk assessments, and this would have been a direct conflict of interest because I might lose or be perceived as having lost my objectivity had I assisted them in remediating the identified gaps.

After leaving my previous firm, I took the opportunity to reach out to the CISO and simply stated, "For a long time, you have asked me if I could help you resolve the issues we identified in your information security program. Would you be interested in me coming on as a consultant and helping you in addressing those issues?" The answer was immediate, "Yes!" Within twenty-four hours we had a handshake agreement on the scope of work. Afterward, the CISO shared his reasoning, stating that I had always been an objective and yet collaborative partner, able to effectively communicate with his executive management team.

In my new role, I reported directly to the CISO with a dotted line to the CIO. True to our prior relationship, we collaboratively developed their system-wide remediation plan, capital budget, and most importantly, their board proposal presentation—a presentation that outlined our plan, the million dollars–plus investment required, and a request for executive approval. After gaining the necessary board approvals, I found myself in an impromptu debrief with the CIO and CISO. The CIO was a very thoughtful leader and not one to waste words; however, at one point he interrupted our conversation to share his gratitude for the knowledge and support I had provided and told me that I was "part of the team."

As my firm's first consulting client, I found this to be a very powerful experience and life lesson. For years, my previous firm had been the sole provider of internal audit services for this client. In my role, I was responsible for overseeing the execution of a wide variety of technology and operational assessments. Frequently, as with any highly-effective risk management function, my teams would identify critically high-risk issues demanding management's attention. Despite the tension these types of discoveries frequently create with a client's management team, it was the approach I had chosen to use in framing and communicating our findings that allowed me to maintain a mutually respectful relationship and generally positive rapport with their executives—an unintentional byproduct that directly impacted my future success.

Over the next six years at my firm, I am humbled to share that I never once was required to sell a consulting engagement. Each opportunity came as a result of my reputation, a personal relationship, or an unsolicited referral. I attribute this to empathy and my ability to manage the fallout of a decision, turning what historically would have been a negative conversation into a positive learning and development opportunity.

Wrapping up this personal aside, I will share with you that I am always humbled to receive an unexpected referral for a new business opportunity based on a previous working relationship or my reputation. It's not that I lack confidence, but more that I'm truly grateful and genuinely touched to know I have had such a positive impact on someone that I would rise to the top of their recommendation list. What I found most surprising was that most of the referrals I received came from either an employee who I had to let go or a client to whom I had previously delivered a damning audit report to their management team. It's these experiences that I have been truly moved by, and the impact we can have by approaching these types of situations with grace and empathy.

Legacy

In decision-making, I feel that your ability to manage fallout is the most important factor contributing to your personal legacy, well-being, and relationship management.

Have you ever had someone reach out to you years after an event, only to thank you for the impact you had on their life? The first time this happened to me, it was a contractor I had hired to help me with an information security department transformation project. This was a person of few emotional words; however, he took the time to explain where he was at that point in his life when I'd hired him, how that role I had given him had played a pivotal impact on his life, and that he was forever grateful for the opportunity I had given him. Subsequently, after working for me, he was hired by one of my clients, which only further extended the financial and personal security he needed to establish a strong financial foundation for the rest of his life.

To me, there is no greater compliment to your character and the life you have chosen, than to receive a compliment like this. Looking decades into the future, I would absolutely prefer to sit back in a rocking chair reflecting on the number of lives I have enriched, rather than swimming in the wealth accumulated throughout my career without regard for the harm I had caused. The ironic thing is that the actions and activities which contribute to building a strong and positive legacy are the same ones that contribute to your personal success, business relationships, and often your career trajectory.

Self-Study Questions:

- Have you sufficiently assessed and accounted for those who will be impacted by the outcome of your decision?
- For those impacted, have you identified those who will be negatively affected and how, such as a loss of employment, shift in role and responsibilities, or reassignment, requiring relocation?
- What responsibilities do you have in managing the fallout of a decision, whether or not it was yours to make?
- If one is required, have you developed a formal communication or change management plan to assist in managing the outcome of a decision?

PRINCIPLE 7:
PRACTICE SELF-REFLECTION

An Acute **Sense of Self-Awareness**
Empowers Personal Growth

"It's fine to celebrate success, but it's more important to heed the lessons of failure."

—BILL GATES

Have you ever looked back on a decision and admitted to yourself that despite your best intention, you did not make the right choice— or at least selected the best one available—whether it was due to a lack of information-gathering, analysis, personal bias, impulsiveness, or one of a litany of other reasons? Of course, you have. We all have.

Self-admittedly, I am a student of hard knocks, meaning that the most impressionable lessons I have learned in my life and career were those that I experienced firsthand. During my years of working in risk management, I have found decision-making was no different. Assessing your past experiences and incorporating those lessons learned into your decision-making process is a critical step in personal development and your ability to evolve into a confident and decisive leader.

The practice of self-reflection dates back thousands of years, quoted, referenced, and defined in various forms by countless philosophers, theologians, and now businesspeople. It entails the process of taking an introspective assessment of your conscious self, purposefully focusing on one's thoughts, feelings, attitudes, beliefs, and actions. Yet, there are many additional areas we can choose to focus on and apply what we have learned to our present and future selves.

Examples of questions to ask yourself:
- The past: "What caused me to do that?"
- The present: "Why am I doing this?"
- The future: "What should I do and why?"

The practice of self-reflection, as defined by clinical psychologist and author Nick Wignall is "the ability to pay attention to your own thoughts, emotions, decisions, and behaviors. While it's good to be self-reflective about what happened in the past, it's better to be able to use self-reflection in real-time to improve your decisions and behavior."[25]

Admittedly, I do not practice self-reflection as frequently as I would like to these days, and this is why it remains a permanent fixture on my list of personal goals, a goal that became a primary driver for writing this book. As I have shared before, my family is my priority and North Star. Observing my daughters and the social challenges they periodically faced at school, I found myself often thinking, "why would someone do that?" It was by carrying that thought over to my experiences in risk management that it struck me—most, if not all issues we found in our client's organizational and risk assessments were rooted in, or the result of, a poor decision or an ineffective decision-making process. Again, I often found myself asking, "why would someone do that?"

Personal Development

Why is self-reflection such a critical component of successful decision-making? It wasn't by accident that I added self-reflection as the seventh and last principle to my framework. It is the principle that serves to assist us in developing and refining each of the aforementioned principles. Pausing for a moment to revisit the notions that most of us were never formally taught how to make a decision and our access to mentors is steadily declining, has made self-reflection the last line of defense in identifying our personal development needs. It is an opportunity to assess how our thoughts and actions might have negatively impacted the outcome of a decision, and then identify the fundamental skills necessary to cultivate personal growth; which in this case is the ability to make an effective decision.

Adopting an effective self-reflection process where you proactively document, analyze, and apply your lessons learned to future decisions will, over the course of time, produce better outcomes and yield higher-quality results. Self-reflection provides us with critical insights into how well we executed in making an important decision and identify opportunities where we can improve, which in many cases might have been otherwise overlooked. While this sounds relatively simple, without discipline, we are often destined to make the same mistakes over and over.

As I have shared openly, I was not born with the requisite skills to make an effective decision that consistently produced productive outcomes, and have made my fair share of poor ones. And yet in the infancy of my personal growth, I recognized that decision-making would be one of the, if not the *most*, crucial executive skills determining my success and legacy. I won't sugarcoat it though; early on, I found the practice frequently broke me down emotionally and physically. Similar to standing in front of a mirror naked, observing and analyzing each and every flaw you have can become an overwhelming exercise.

Decision Journal

As fortune would have it, though I was gifted with many talents, recollection was not one of them. A practical way to cultivate openness is to keep a decision journal. If you are like me, a journal is a requisite tool and an effective method for recalling your decisions and how you chose to consider, contemplate, and collaborate with others, as well as the feelings you experienced throughout the process. In addition, it provides you the ability to reflect on your results and if there were opportunities for you to improve your decision-making skill set.

A decision journal can take a lot of different forms, anything from a Google document to a cheap notebook. When you are faced with a significant decision, simply spend a few minutes chronicling your thoughts on the decision you were presented with, the factors you choose to consider, the challenges and impediments that you faced, and your final decision. After which, take the time to revisit your notes and document the resulting outcome, including whether you achieved your goal, and why. It's by proactively documenting the lessons you learned in the process, that you will begin to train yourself to identify influences, biases, and other impediments, and how they impact your ability to make an effective decision. This will allow you to implement tools and techniques that help to improve your ability to make effective decisions that will consistently produce better outcomes.

In the case of self-reflection, we often initially see nothing but our shortcomings. There is hope though. I found that by taking an intentional and consistent approach, you will start to observe small incremental changes that result in better outcomes for your decisions. Using the body image analogy, it is those small successes that will instill you with newfound confidence and personal drive, which will prove to be a catalyst for continued growth. For me, it was knowing that I had taken the right steps and selected the best option available which then created an endorphin-like rush, as I became increasingly confident in myself and the decisions I made on a daily basis.

Continuing with the body transformation analogy, personal growth through self-reflection requires dedication, consistency, and personal sacrifice. Dedication is the personal acknowledgment and resolve that to grow, you must evolve into your better self. Consistency is maintaining a regular practice of self-reflection that provides you with the feedback necessary to identify opportunities and flaws within your standard routines, as well as enables you to measure personal growth. Personal sacrifice is being comfortable with being uncomfortable, after recognizing the harmful effects your habits might have had on your success and the well-being of others. By recognizing these factors you will develop a clearer understanding of the change, effort, and investment required for personal growth and the ability to make more effective decisions.

An unspoken secret of self-reflection is that deliberate application of this principle will serve to expedite the speed at which you are able to incorporate it within your decision-making process. Quickly, you will learn to apply the lessons you have learned in the moment, if not before you are asked to make a decision.

For example, in a moment of self-reflection, you recognize that you frequently move straight into problem-solving, and do not stop to fully listen to the feedback and concerns shared by others. With this in mind, it's in the midst of a difficult employee performance review that you begin to notice a growing sense of personal pride about the guidance you are sharing, but also observe that the employee has become increasingly retracted and defensive. Being mindful of the aforementioned goal of listening before problem-solving, you pause what you are saying and ask for their input and feedback, all the while resisting the urge to interrupt until they have been able to share their perspective.

A small and subtle shift in how you navigate what is often a difficult conversation, and yet it will have an enormous impact in how your feedback will be received by others. By demonstrating empathy, the team member is far more likely to understand and accept the feedback on their performance. In addition, you cultivate a bidirectional bridge of trust, by providing an opportunity to receive direct feedback. In some cases, valuable insights come from the employee's feedback on how you are perceived and opportunities for personal development and growth. How many high-performing organizations would have better outcomes if they had given their executives 10 percent more capacity for real-time self-reflection, so they could apply it to the ways in which they manage and make decisions?

It goes without saying that dynamic and high-growth organizations would receive the greatest benefit from adopting the practice of real-time self-reflection, as their objectives would be based on an ability to be nimble and react in real time to grow their business. The key to cultivating self-reflection as a core attribute of an organization's culture and potentially even a competitive advantage is how you engage and nurture a positive environment for employees to think critically about their decisions. Employees who are able to react and respond to decisions in the moment are far more effective and valuable than those who would have otherwise deferred a decision, which might have unintentionally undermined an outcome you sought to achieve.

How to Cultivate Real-Time Self-Reflection

In his book *Mindsight: The New Science of Personal Transformation*, Dan Siegel uses the metaphor of a camera to explain self-reflection: "The better the camera and clearer the lens, the more accurate the final photo will be. But as any good photographer will tell you, to get the clearest image possible, you must use a tripod to stabilize the camera and the lens, since even small vibrations and movements can distort the final image. Most of us have the basic equipment for self-reflection, a decent camera, and lens, so to speak. However, to bring our powers of self-reflection to the next level, we need to cultivate three specific skills that contribute to the habit of self-reflection: openness, observation, and objectivity."[26]

Openness

Openness is the ability to listen, observe, and engage without prejudgement or bias. When we demonstrate openness, we allow ourselves to see things for what they are without placing a filter or preconceived notion about what they ought to be. Instead, we take the opportunity to observe individuals, situations, and decisions for what they are, which includes both internal and external factors.

Years ago, I had a consultant on my team who was a stellar resource, who aspired to climb the consulting career ladder and become a partner at our firm. Over the course of time, we became close, and I eventually took over the role of his formal career coach. As with anyone whom I coached, I would initially inquire what were their personal and professional career aspirations. In the case of this individual, his immediate focus and obvious priority was his career. "Jack, I want to be just like you. I want to learn and grow here at the firm so that I can one day become a partner."

At no point did he share his personal life aspirations or even family background. As his coach, I wanted to also understand his personal drivers and therefore inquired about his personal goals and his family. It was at this point that he shared that the relationship with his wife was strained, due to him spending extensive amounts of time on the road for work. Even when he wasn't on the road, he would put in long hours at the office. Furthermore, he shared that his children were becoming emotionally distant, because he was not home and able to help with their homework, attend their sporting events, etc. As a result, he expressed concerns about the future of his marriage and relationships with his children. I followed up and asked what kind of relationship he wanted with his wife and kids. He shared that he wanted the love and passion he once had with his wife. He also desperately wanted to rekindle the close bond he once had with his children, a kind of relationship where his kids would run into his arms whenever he walked through the front door.

Seeing the divergence between his professional and personal aspirations, I asked why he prioritized his career over his family. A key piece to his answer rested on the influence of his parents and preconditioned ideas for what constitutes a successful career. While these can be strong motivators for some, they can also place undue pressure upon an individual. His parents had placed an emphasis on his being a strong and stable financial provider, and, therefore, he had sought a career in accounting at a global firm that would provide him with both.

After peeling back the layers of his inherited biases, his own values began to become clearer, which allowed him to shift his focus to his own needs and begin to cultivate his own sense of what he and his family wanted from his career. He began making decisions for himself, rather than the preconceived values and thoughts instilled throughout his upbringing. As a result, not only did his spirits lift, but eventually, he chose to leave the demanding and fast-paced world of consulting.

After much consideration, he carefully assessed his options and decided to accept a stable corporate position near his home, allowing him to spend more time with his family. With a newfound shift in how he approached life, he decided that he wanted to have a greater and more positive influence on the world. By evaluating his options, he concluded that law was the optimal path and earned a Juris Doctor degree, subsequently passing the bar exam on his first attempt, and is now practicing family law. It was at this point that he reached back out to me to share his success, his appreciation for the direction I had provided, and the fulfillment he was able to create for both himself and, more importantly, his family.

Observation

Most of us might associate observation with watching other people, events, or objects. In the capacity of decision-making, observation refers to the ability to view and process your own actions in the same way you do external objects and events. As a component of self-reflection, this skill is especially helpful in identifying and correcting poor or unproductive habits.

For some, especially those who consider themselves in the realm of a "type A" personality, an example of a bad habit might be the compulsion to say yes to every request. While you might believe that doing so makes one indispensable (thus accelerating their rise up the corporate ladder), it ultimately has the effect of causing an overextension of oneself. As a result, their work product often suffers, creating the exact opposite public perception of what they sought to achieve. It is far better to do superlative work in one area than to do shoddy work in many.

In particular, I recall a senior consultant on my team who was a lifelong overachiever and who also succumbed to the addiction of saying, "yes." After building up an adequate level of trust with her, she shared that early in life she had become a single mother prior to attending college. Despite this early wrinkle in life, she was determined to provide and be a role model for her children. She went on to share that she graduated with a degree from the University of Southern California, while simultaneously holding down a full-time job. Throughout this process, she had made it her personal goal that she would outwork her peers to climb the corporate ladder. I was taken aback, as this level of commitment and work ethic is an extremely rare quality I have found in our next generation of leaders.

Several months into a project, as part of a standard performance feedback session, I shared that the quality of her work and overall performance was beginning to deteriorate. Recognized as a reliable and high-performing resource, she would constantly get bombarded with requests from her clients, team members, and the partners/directors who oversaw each of her projects. As a result, she was overcommitted and it wound up impacting the quality and level of attention she was able to give to each project.

She shared that her goal was to get promoted to manager that year, and she therefore feared the consequences of turning down a project and how she would be perceived. Her anxiety about saying no was not founded on actual facts or feedback, but derived from her internal thinking that she would be labeled as lazy, slow, or not a team player. A surprising revelation, as I found her to be a tremendous leader who was able to effectively manage her teams and handle difficult client situations with ease. And yet, she had the compulsion to say yes to new requests received from her partners and directors.

The real problem, she explained, was that in addition to being overwhelmed with the constant flow of requests, she was falling farther and farther behind in her work paper review queue and, therefore, impacting the productivity of the entire team. On one hand, I was upset with how she had put herself (and her projects) at risk; however, I understood the emotions that were driving her behaviors.

It was then that I suggested she write down a list of all the commitments she had been assigned or had agreed to. She initially thought it sounded like a waste of time—especially when she already had so much to do—and was hesitant to try it. Finally, I told her, "I think your propensity to say yes is driven by the belief that saying no may negatively impact your career trajectory. However, you must understand that in the world of consulting, quality is far more important than quantity." By understanding your commitments and capacity, you will be far more prepared to either turn down new requests or request for additional support.

She acquiesced and agreed to "give it a shot," as my explanation seemed to have convinced her that the velocity she was operating at wasn't sustainable and the benefits of delivering a higher quality work product would have a far greater impact on her aspirations to get promoted. Over time, she was able to gain a better understanding of her commitments and negative thought patterns about how she felt others would perceive her if she turned down a request. Armed with a new sense of awareness enabled her to have open conversations with the leaders she reported to, able to manage her emotions and a natural propensity to say yes. As a result, she developed a stronger personal conviction about how to respond to these types of requests in a more thoughtful and confident manner. This change in her psyche was due in large part to her mindfulness practice.

It's during high-pressure situations that we often become anxious and stressed, we often are inflicted with self-doubt about our capabilities, decisions, and the manner a potentially unsavory conclusion will have on the recipient. As the aforementioned highlights, we tend to make poor decisions when we don't take the time to properly assess the information available and properly evaluate our options. Nick Wignall pointedly summarizes this by sharing that the key to making better decisions during these types of situations "is to be able to turn our attention inward and better understand what factors are really driving our choices and behaviors."[27]

Objectivity

Objectivity is the ability to separate and assess facts, perceptions, or conditions from our identity and personal beliefs, feelings, and biases. This is particularly true when you are feeling judged and backed into a corner. It's during these times that it's critical to recognize that your feelings of anxiety and self-doubt are based on a distorted lens of reality, which we are innately conditioned to assume the worst. Incorporating objectivity into the decision-making process allows you to take a step back and objectively assess the facts available, identify missing information, and define what actions are necessary to make a confident conclusion and decision. Your beliefs, feelings, and biases are valid considerations you should assess, but they frequently don't paint the complete picture of reality.

This was a trait I saw manifested firsthand while working as an independent consultant for a health care system for which I'd been engaged to assist with their selection and implementation of a new medical records and revenue management system. It was a high-profile program and it was my sponsor, their senior vice president of IT, whom I found to suffer from the negative implications of self-doubt. The implementation, combined with the client's culture, proved fertile ground to induce a lack of objectivity, as interestingly enough the implementation had received mixed interest and support from the client's executive leadership team, despite it being a critical component of their growth strategy.

In my role, I often attended their weekly executive leadership meetings, which was atypical of the organization's culture. After several of these meetings, I observed that my client sponsor periodically struggled with delivering status updates on the project, as he suffered from intrusive and insecure thoughts. As evidence of this, following my first meeting with their leadership team, he spontaneously initiated a sidebar conversation. It was then that he shared his concerns about the views of influential executives, particularly those whom he believed questioned his ability to deliver on the program. Despite having the requisite knowledge, experience, and successful track record of having led similar programs of this magnitude, he assumed the worst.

Believing there were bad actors seeking to undermine the project, he began to question his ability to effectively communicate and navigate the executive corridors, and, therefore, was somehow more likely to fail. As you might imagine, these types of thought patterns caused a tremendous amount of stress and anxiety, which, as a result, caused strains on his relationships with his team, vendors, and me. So much so that he would inexplicitly call out individuals behind their backs as being incompetent or unreliable. Due to his unfettered focus on the project at hand, he wasn't able to enjoy the personal working relationships he had so cherished before. To quell his fears, we often held private debriefs following these executive meetings, where I was asked to critique the meeting, as well as his performance, and if I'd picked up on any negative reactions or adverse facial expressions.

While I had not been hired to be an executive coach, I understood that the success of the project was directly tied to this executive's ability to effectively navigate the political landscape, and this included cultivating trusted relationships with his peers. He was truly a strong, knowledgeable, and accomplished executive; however, like many of us, he allowed his lack of objectivity to create a crippling sense of self-doubt. I helped him to actively assess the project status and forthcoming needs, in order to practice the skill of separating his fears from the task at hand. As a result, we successfully accomplished the goals of the project and he regained his confidence as an executive leader, able to cultivate and maintain the types of collegial and fulfilling relationships he valued.

Whether you're battling intrusive thoughts, or simply experiencing difficulty separating your personal biases from a professional environment, we all struggle at times to acknowledge, express, and share our emotions. Consequently, both our mental health and professional performance can suffer. To improve your ability to remain objective when it matters, try incorporating your thoughts in the aforementioned decision journal and thereby allow yourself to take a step back and properly assess the situation so you can make the most productive choices available to you.

Using Siegel's analogy, highlighting the necessity of openness, observation, and objectivity as the cornerstones of an effective self-reflective process, reminds us of the importance of actively listening to feedback, recognizing the efforts of others, and the necessity of mindfully blocking personal predispositions and biases. Collectively, these cornerstones will enable you to achieve more productive and consistently successful outcomes.

By adopting an effective self-reflection process where you proactively document, analyze, and apply your lessons learned to future decisions will, over time, produce better outcomes and yield higher-quality results. Self-reflection provides us with critical insights on how well we executed in making an important decision and identifying opportunities on how we can improve, which in many cases might have been otherwise overlooked. While sounding relatively simple, without discipline, we are often destined to make the same mistakes over and over.

Self-Study Questions:

- Did I achieve the outcome I sought to accomplish? If not, what did I observe as the contributing factors?
- Regardless of the outcome, how could I have improved the path taken?
- For positive outcomes, could I have approached my decision in a different manner that would have made the process more efficient and further nurtured key relationships?
- Throughout the process, were there opportunities for me to collaborate or empower others? Did I take the opportunity to include these individuals, as a means of developing deeper and more productive relationships?
- Did I compromise my integrity in an effort to achieve a predefined expectation, timeline, or expected outcome?

CONCLUSION

Confident and Decisive Leaders Require
Advocacy *and* Education

> *"A director makes 100 decisions an hour ... If you don't know how to make the right decision, you're not a director."*
> **— GEORGE LUCAS**

Workplace-related stress and anxiety are real, and we have a shared responsibility to address the contributing factors. Having spent the last twenty-plus years consulting in risk management and working alongside executive leaders from across a variety of industries, as well as holding senior roles in technology, I will tell you that decision-making is, by far, one of the most stressful aspects of business I have consistently found with my clients and teams.

A Crisis in the Making

What I find particularly concerning is that the percentage of our workforce who suffer from work-related stress and anxiety is increasing, a trend that I fear will continue for the foreseeable future. An observation confirmed by Forbes' 2022 Leadership Study found that "rates of anger, anxiety, and aggression are accelerating—for the third consecutive year." [28] It is clear that the mounting pressures of a constantly evolving work environment have and will continue to contribute to the toll on our workforce.

Whether it is the frequency with which we are changing jobs, the adoption of an increasingly transient and remote workforce, or the ever-present influence and addiction to technology, we feel more isolated than ever before. And yet we as leaders are being asked to consume information and make critical decisions at what often seems to be unattainable speeds. Supporting this notion, Gallup's 2022 workforce poll reported that, "44% of the world's employees experienced anxiety, anger, and/or sadness a lot of the previous day."[29]

Workplace stress, specifically around decision-making, is a brewing mental health crisis of epidemic proportions that has not been isolated as a critical business risk and prioritized by organizations around the world. Despite the overwhelming evidence of the benefits that decision-related training and mentoring provide, our current and future leaders receive virtually no hands-on training or mentoring on how to make important decisions, which, historically, was the primary approach used for education and personal development.

There is a solution though. Recognizing that the structure and needs of our workforce are continuously evolving, it's incumbent upon us to adapt and implement techniques that reflect each "new norm." Recognize that every individual and organization has a unique set of needs as a result of their environment and external influences. However, the fundamental stages of decision-making—and recognition that it is a process, not an event—are the critical elements for consistently making better decisions that result in a higher percentage of positive outcomes. Stemming from the personal investment I had made in myself and in observing the anxiety and stress many endure in making decisions on a daily basis was the premise for which I developed the *7 Principles of Successful Decision-Making.*

Making effective decisions that consistently produce positive outcomes is both an art and a science. It can be a formal process, comprised of distinctive stages that require continuous interpretation and consideration due to the ever-constant variability of inputs we are presented with. It might also be a fluid process that flexes to the needs and priorities of a given situation, audience, or external factors well beyond our control. Finding balance in how decision-making is approached is the essence of what makes a leader successful and able to confidently make decisions knowing they have clearly defined their objectives, asked the right questions, and established a plan that will enable them to accomplish their goals.

I have tremendous compassion and empathy for those of you who have suffered from the anxiety and self-doubt decision-making often creates, simply due to a lack of knowledge or understanding of a process to help guide you through the necessary steps to make the right conclusion. As many of you can relate, I frequently navigated many of life's difficult decisions by putting up a false armor of confidence that served to hide my fears and insecurities. As a result, I can recall virtually every important decision I have ever made, not because of the outcome, but rather the emotional toll that it took on me.

The Gift

Please give yourself the gift of evaluating the process taken in making a decision and refrain from simply judging yourself, or others, based on outcomes alone.

EPILOGUE

It was 8:00 a.m. on a fall day in 2002. I was a 27-year-old senior associate employed by one of the largest accounting firms in the world and found myself sitting outside the doors of my first executive committee meeting.

Yes, it was an unusual ask for a staff member to present a client's executive leadership team with the summarized results of an assessment we'd performed; however, this was an unusual scenario where the results of our assessment would be unsettling for both the client as well as our firm. Sitting next to me, a tenured accounting partner repeatedly asked me, "Are you ready?" I wondered if he was more nervous than I was. He had invited me to this meeting because it was his client and, self-admittedly, he was not adept at explaining the risk implications posed to the organization as a result of a series of poor management decisions. He did, however, fully understand the implications their management team faced, which could have significant financial and regulatory consequences for the organization. No pressure here. I was simultaneously electrified and terrified.

On deck to deliver the next presentation, a damning one, I had been asked to present an executive summary of the organizational risks my team had identified as part of an assessment performed on the client's internal controls and administrative processes responsible for protecting their most critical information systems. It was a standard technology assessment performed by our firm, generally in conjunction with a client's annual financial audit. What had we discovered?

The client at hand was a regional health care system, who had failed to implement multiple layers of critical information security configurations and administrative controls, simply due to poor decisions made by the client's management team. The most brazen of which was that the director of IT had been provisioned administrator access to their medical records, revenue, and accounting systems, along with virtually every other critical application platform utilized by the health care system. Compounding their risk, this individual's accounts were configured to circumvent the organization's security policy and did not require a password to log in. Therefore, anyone who gained access to their desktop had unfettered access to view, change, and delete virtually any dataset, including the audit logs. Further, we observed that this individual would often leave their office door open during the day, as well as after they had left for the evening. When my team inquired why they had been granted exceptions to the security policy, their explanation focused on emergency scenarios where access delays could encumber their ability to effectively respond. Meanwhile, we also uncovered that the same person did not have the knowledge or background to effectively navigate or configure these systems, making the previous statement a moot point. Lack of passwords or even leaving their office door unlocked were justified as "making it easier" to do their job.

The health care system, similar to many other public and private companies, had issued public bonds and financial agreements, each of which was subject to debt covenants. Debt covenants are conditional terms included within a lending agreement memorializing performance expectations of the borrower's operational and financial performance responsibilities. Simply put, despite being a not-for-profit entity, they were still responsible for maintaining effective internal governance and were required to deliver an annual opinion on its financial performance and the effectiveness of its internal controls. Should you breach a debt covenant, the penalties can be harsh. A company might lose access to financing, see an increased cost to borrow money, or be met with financial penalties. This is because the lender is trying to mitigate their risk, and breaching a covenant shows that you have introduced new risks to the organization that could negatively impact performance and the ability to repay the debt obligation.

How did we get here? As previously mentioned, I was a senior associate within my firm's risk assurance division, and three months prior I was transferred into their health industries group and assigned seven new clients. As you would expect, each client I was given was someone else's hand-me-down, or as I called them, rough-cut gems from the firm's vast list of prestigious clients. New to each client account, in preparation for this year's audit I reviewed the prior year's working papers to help familiarize myself.

At the time, the rigor and standards used by accounting firms to prepare for these types of reviews often varied by the individual leading the assessment. Generally speaking, a team lead would take one of two approaches. The first assumed that the prior year's work was correctly scoped and executed. Based on this assumption, you requested similar supporting documents as the previous year, updated the details and dates of your testing procedures, confirmed the conclusions, wrapped up your work papers, and issued the final report. The second approach was more deliberate and, therefore, more time-consuming, as the process would take into consideration the previous year's work as well as new risks posed to the organization.

As my first time working with this client and being assigned the lead auditor role, I was responsible for the outcome of our work and chose the second approach. Prefacing the focus of my analysis,

I had just rolled off a yearlong engagement where we implemented a new information security program for a financial services firm to enhance the protection of their clients' accounts. Well attuned to the risks posed by a soft security posture, I decided that one area of focus for this year's assessment would be our client's information security controls. By focusing on their information security program, it became quickly evident that they had not implemented the necessary controls to protect their organization's data and ensure the results produced by their medical records and financial systems were accurate.

Come again? We've got a BIG problem.

After immediately notifying my risk management partner, other partners were asked to cross-review our work. In each case, they agreed with the procedures performed and our final conclusions. The problem? Our firm had signed off on the client's internal controls for years, and each of the gaps identified had been in place for multiple years. My presentation that morning involved two parts: first, a summary of the internal controls tested in support of the annual financial audit, and second, a summary of what we found, along with the risks posed to the organization.

As you would expect, the information I presented landed like a lead balloon. Silence initially, followed by a vigorous discussion on how the organization would respond. Seeing that the debt covenants focused on financial controls, several management-level account reconciliations were identified and utilized by our firm's partner to substantiate that the organization had sufficient governance to support the accuracy of the financial numbers reported. The kicker for me: patient and financial records access controls were not a contingency tied to the health care system's debt covenants and, therefore, not included in their remediation plan.

As I viewed the situation, I saw two failures. First, the organization had pervasive issues with its decision-making processes, highlighted by a glaring knowledge gap, embedded biases, insufficient collaboration, and an absent vision for the Information Systems department. Further, the Information Systems management team was unaware of their debt covenant requirements, nor had the finance and accounting executives appropriately informed their executives of their expectations. They had also made numerous decisions that compromised the integrity of their information systems and, ultimately, their business. The second failure was a systematic breakdown within our firm's planning and internal review processes, an inherent confirmation bias about the reliability and quality of work performed by the prior year's team, which in this instance had overlooked new emerging risks created by poor decisions made by our client's management team.

As previously mentioned, this was the first of seven existing clients I had been assigned to that year. While each organization had passed its prior year's assessment, this would become the first of several presentations I would be asked to deliver that fall—each due to inadequate controls over the organization's information systems.

During my time working in risk management, I have observed one consistent theme: that better decisions lead to better outcomes. The challenge presented by this is, of course, what constitutes a good decision? How can one be confident that they have sufficiently assessed the information available to make the most appropriate decision to achieve the intended outcome? For many, the answer is unclear.

ACKNOWLEDGMENTS

"The happiest people don't have the best of everything, they just make the best of everything they have." A profound and life-changing philosophy I embraced during a particularly turbulent period, which forever altered how I viewed life and the decisions I would be asked to make. If there is one final wish that I can bestow upon this world, it is to always look for the positive in any given moment, situation, and most importantly the accompanying decisions you will be asked to make.

To my wife Shannon: you are forever my angel without wings. Your unconditional love and unwavering faith gave me the support I needed to chase our dreams. What were fragments of our imaginations over 27 years ago are now a reality, laying the foundation for even greater aspirations and life adventures. There are no words to describe the love, affection, and appreciation I have for you and the sacrifices you have made for our family. Without you, *The Decision Switch* would never have been written.

To my daughters, Makenna and Sienna: you never cease to amaze me with your inner strength, personal resilience, and compassion for others. You were my inspiration for taking a leap of faith and authoring a book about setting goals, navigating the challenges life will throw at you, and knowing how to make the types of decisions that will enable you to achieve your personal ambitions. Despite the countless hours Daddy escaped into his office, pouring his heart into this book, I am forever grateful for the additional time it gave me to spend with you and watch you grow into strong young women. Remember this, I will forever be your big daddy, always waiting for you with open arms and so long as I am able to do so, will throw you up in the air just so I can hear you scream "WHEEEEE", as you fall back to earth.

To my mother and father: it was you who instilled the values of hard work, personal character, and positive thinking that proceeded to take me farther in life than even my loftiest expectations. Watching firsthand your struggles in building a family business without a viable safety net, having the personal integrity to persevere while incumbents tried to tear you down, and filling our house with ever-present voices of positive and motivational speakers like Wayne Dyer, Norman Vincent Peale, Zig Ziglar, and a young Tony Robbins—from your vast collection of well-worn cassette tapes. While you self-admittedly shared that you were unprepared for parenthood, you taught me that actions speak louder than words. I love you both and while you might not have always initially agreed with my decisions, I am eternally grateful for the endless support you have shown me.

To my brother Mike: I admittedly don't say it often enough, but I love you. I am forever grateful for the example you set for me at a very young age, and you still continue to be one of the most prominent and inspirational figures in my life today. Not just as an older brother, but as a role model who demonstrated the indelible qualities of love, leadership, integrity, work ethic, empathy, and most importantly what it takes to be an incredible husband, father, and friend.

To the insightful mentors, who patiently took me under their wing and helped me develop the character traits required of a well-rounded leader. Each left a unique and indelible mark, the most consistent of which was that true leaders never measure success by the value of their bank account, but by the number of lives they have personally touched and positively impacted over the course of their careers. To name but just a few of those who made a difference in my life include Dr. Helen Rothberg, Cliff Papish, Vincent Catalanotto, A. Michael Smith, Jason Emmons, and David Maberry.

To my friends and extended family: I frequently remind myself that the most accurate reflection of ourselves are the individuals we are blessed to have in our lives. A lengthy list and a truly humbling thought, based on the circle I have been fortunate enough to keep over the course of my life. Recognize that we hold tiny pieces of each other, whether it's an interest, experience, habit, or simply a comforting embrace; it's these relationships that I will forever value and be grateful for the impact you had on my life.

To my writing partner Sarah Sheppeck and editor Ronald Klier, I am forever grateful for the knowledge, guidance, and patience you imparted throughout this process, which enabled me to bring this vision to life. Without question, your insights and suggestions helped to mold the structure and shape the messaging included within *The Decision Switch*. It was your coaching that allowed me to translate the abstract and often-misunderstood executive skill of decision-making into a valuable reference tool for today's leaders, using storytelling to bring each principle to life. From the bottom of my heart, thank you.

To my publishing consultant Janica Smith: you are a beacon of light in the often complex and opaque world of publishing. Carefully guiding me through each challenging twist and turn, with an unmistakable sense of calm and confidence. I cannot thank you enough for your patience and support throughout the publishing process.

To Shola Richards: had it not been for that fateful summer evening, while watching our daughters play in the backyard, we talked at length about self-fulfillment by giving back, I would have never been compelled to write this book. "But, what if?" A simple question you repeatedly asked every time I dismissed the idea, proved to be the catalyst I needed. You are an inspiration to many, yet one of the most humble, kind, and generous human beings whom I have the fortune to call a close friend. I am forever grateful for your mentoring, motivation, and unconditional support throughout this process.

And finally, to my daily writing partner: Sophie our portly French Bulldog. A stalwart member of the family, named after a character in one of my daughters' favorite books. They would have never forgiven me had I not acknowledged her and the unconditional love she has brought into our home. Fondly, you were my constant companion throughout this journey, always ready to afford me with an affectionate smile or provide the levity I needed during the writing process.

ENDNOTES

1. "Countrywide Eases Target for Growth." Bloomberg News. March 25, 2005. https://www.latimes.com/archives/la-xpm-2005-may-25-fi-country25-story.html.

2. Lang, Susan S. "'Mindless Autopilot' Drives People to Dramatically Underestimate How Many Daily Food Decisions They Make, Cornell Study Finds." *Cornell Chronicle*, December 22, 2006. https://news.cornell.edu/stories/2006/12/mindless-autopilot-drives-people-underestimate-food-decisions.

3. Rollings, Mike. "Effective Decision Making Must Be Connected, Contextual and Continuous." Gartner. October 12, 2021. https://www.gartner.com/smarterwithgartner/how-to-make-better-business-decisions.

4. "A World of Discovery." *Innovation Quarterly*. Boeing, May 2018. https://www.boeing.com/features/innovation-quarterly/may2018/feature-thought-leadership-hyslop.page.

5. Isidore, Chris. "These Are the Mistakes That Cost Boeing CEO Dennis Muilenburg His Job | CNN Business." CNN. December 24, 2019. https://www.cnn.com/2019/12/24/business/boeing-dennis-muilenburg-mistakes/index.html.

6. Kolmar, Chris. "Average Number of Jobs in a Lifetime [2022]: All Statistics." Zippia Average Number of Jobs in a Lifetime 2022 All Statistics Comments. April 5, 2022. https://www.zippia.com/advice/average-number-jobs-in-lifetime/.

7. Gandhi, Vipula, and Jennifer Robinson. "The 'Great Resignation' Is Really the 'Great Discontent.'" Gallup.com. November 11, 2022. https://www.gallup.com/workplace/351545/great-resignation-really-great-discontent.aspx.

8. Skarr, Douglas. Issue brief. The Fundamentals of Interest Rate Swaps. Sacramento, CA: California Debt and Investment Advisory Commission, 2004. https://www.treasurer.ca.gov/cdiac/reports/rateswap04-12.pdf.

9. Garvin, David A., and Michael A. Roberto, "What You Don't Know about Making Decisions." *Harvard Business Review*, August 25, 2015. https://hbr.org/2001/09/what-you-dont-know-about-making-decisions.

10. Garvin, David A., and Michael A. Roberto, "What You Don't Know about Making Decisions." *Harvard Business Review*, August 25, 2015. https://hbr.org/2001/09/what-you-dont-know-about-making-decisions.

11. "CDM: Collaborative Decision Making." CDM. Accessed November 12, 2022. https://cdm.fly.faa.gov/.

12. Shepard, Greg. "It's Never Too Early to Establish Your Company's North Star." *Chief Executive*, February 4, 2019. https://chiefexecutive.net/never-establish-company-north-star/.

13. Viscomi, Chiara. "Your Own North Star: Finding Life Purpose and Passion." Meaning, Mind. *HealthyPsych*, January 29, 2019. https://healthypsych.com/your-own-north-star-finding-life-purpose-and-passion/.

14. Harter, Jim. "4 Factors Driving Record-High Employee Engagement in U.S." Workplace. Gallup, December 9, 2022. https://www.gallup.com/workplace/284180/factors-driving-record-high-employee-engagement.aspx.

15. Horntvedt, Jody. "Five Reasons to Involve Others in Public Decisions." UMN Extension. Accessed November 12, 2022. https://extension.umn.edu/public-engagement-strategies/five-reasons-involve-others-public-decisions.

16. "The Ultimate Guide to Running Executive Meetings - 25 Tips from Top Startup Leaders." First Round Review. Accessed October 26, 2022. https://review.firstround.com/the-ultimate-guide-to-running-executive-meetings-25-tips-from-top-startup-leaders.

17. Phillips, Katherine W. "How Diversity Makes Us Smarter." *Greater Good*, September 17, 2018. https://greatergood.berkeley.edu/article/item/how_diversity_makes_us_smarter.

18. Harter, Jim. "4 Factors Driving Record-High Employee Engagement in U.S." Workplace. Gallup, December 9, 2022. https://www.gallup.com/workplace/284180/factors-driving-record-high-employee-engagement.aspx.

19. "U.S. Sales Data." Toy Industry Association. Circana. Accessed January 2023. https://www.toyassociation.org/ta/research/data/u-s-sales-data/toys/research-and-data/data/us-sales-data.aspx.

20. Eurich, Tasha. "95% Of Leaders Think They Have This Quality-but Less than 15% Actually Do." EAB. Daily Briefing, September 27, 2019. https://eab.com/insights/daily-briefing/workplace/leaders-think-they-have-this-quality-but-few-actually-do/.

21. Desmond, Edward W. "What's Ailing Kodak? Fuji While the U.S. Giant Was Sleeping, the Japanese Film Company Cut Prices, Marketed Aggressively, and Now Is Stealing Market Share." CNN Money. October 27, 1997. https://money.cnn.com/magazines/fortune/fortune_archive/1997/10/27/233297/.

22. Sykes, Tom. "Big Projects Might Slip, but Small Steps Win." CIO, April 7, 2022. https://www.cio.com/article/308214/big-projects-might-slip-but-small-steps-win.html.

23. Robinson, Harry. "Why Do Most Transformations Fail? A Conversation with Harry Robinson." Our Insights. McKinsey & Company, July 12, 2019. https://www.mckinsey.com/capabilities/transformation/our-insights/why-do-most-transformations-fail-a-conversation-with-harry-robinson.

24. Goleman, Daniel. *Emotional Intelligence: Why It Can Matter More than IQ.* New York, Bantam Books, 2006.

25. Wignall, Nick. "Know Thyself: 3 Essential Skills for Better Self-Reflection." Emotional Intelligence. Nick Wignall, June 13, 2020. https://nickwignall.com/self-reflection/.

26. Siegel, Daniel J. *Mindsight: The New Science of Personal Transformation.* New York, Bantam Books, 2010.

27. Wignall, Nick. "Know Thyself: 3 Essential Skills for Better Self-Reflection." Emotional Intelligence. Nick Wignall, June 13, 2020. https://nickwignall.com/self-reflection/.

28. Bruce, Jan. "Is Anger and Anxiety in the Workplace the New Normal?" *Forbes Magazine,* August 1, 2022. https://www.forbes.com/sites/janbruce/2022/07/30/is-anger-and-anxiety-in-the-workplace-the-new-normal/.

29. Bruce, Jan. "Is Anger and Anxiety in the Workplace the New Normal?" *Forbes Magazine,* August 1, 2022. https://www.forbes.com/sites/janbruce/2022/07/30/is-anger-and-anxiety-in-the-workplace-the-new-normal/.

INDEX

A

accountability, 20, 80–81
actor-observer bias, 73–75
advocacy-based decision-making, 23–25
air-traffic controllers, 27–28
alternative viewpoints, 50–52, 55–57
Amazon, 45, 46–47
anchoring bias, 69–70
anger, 52, 119–120
annual performance reviews, 24–25
anxiety
    general discussion, 1–2, 14, 119–121
    objectivity and, 113–116
    observation and, 111–113
Apple, 37–38, 66
assessing requests, 27–35
    criticality, 29–30
    dangers of not, 30–34
    knowledge confirmation, 29
    Self-Study Questions, 35
    three-gate evaluation model, 29–30
    value proposition, 30
authority, 85. *See also* roles/responsibilities

B

bad actors
    errors and, 32–33
    general discussion, 14–16
    negative management practices, 54–55
bad decisions, 16–17, 89–101
    anticipating, 90–91
    author personal experience, 96–100
    communication plan, 89–90, 93–96
    empathetic leadership, 92–96
    errors and, 30–34
    from lack of collaboration, 50, 52–53

social skills, 93–96
    underestimating effects, 91
Bank of America, 3
belittling, 54–55
benchmarking, 46–47
bias, 65–77
    actor-observer, 73–75
    anchoring, 69–70
    confirmation, 68–69
    false consensus effect, 71–72
    misinformation effect, 72–73
    overconfidence, 67–68
    self-serving, 75–76
    Self-Study Questions, 77
"Big 4" audit and consulting firms, 61
Boeing, 6–8
bottom-line mentality, 54–55
Bureau of Labor Statistics, 10
buy-in
    champions for developing, 80–81,
        83–84, 85–86
    from stakeholders, 51–52, 55–58

C

CDAOs (chief data and analytics officers), 5
CDM (Collaborative Decision Making)
initiative, 27–28
CFO (chief financial officer), 51–52, 60
champions, 79–87
    accountability and, 20, 80–81
    attributes of effective, 80
    eliminating obstacles, 85
    establishing buy-in, 80–81, 83–84,
        85–86
    false consensus effect and, 71–72
    maintaining momentum, 82–83
    motivating others, 84
    relationship management, 80, 82

ABOUT THE AUTHOR

Jack P. Flaherty is the CEO and Founder of *The Decision Switch*. A former executive officer, strategic advisor, and Big 4 client service executive, who for more than two decades has consulted with many of America's largest corporations. In doing so, he's had the opportunity to oversee hundreds of organizational assessments and conduct thousands of executive interviews and found decision-making to be one of the most critical risks individuals and organizations face on a daily basis.

Based upon his experience and extensive research, he observed many of today's leaders struggle to make important decisions as they were never given the requisite training or mentoring. This reality has been exacerbated by the speed at which business is conducted today, our adoption of hybrid and remote working arrangements, as well as the widespread utilization of real-time communication and collaboration technology platforms.

Recognizing decision-making as one of the most integral executive functions contributing to an individual's and organization's success, he has become an impassioned advocate and has developed a proven framework that educates and transforms individuals into decisive leaders who are able to make decisions confidently at the speed their role requires.

Jack is a leadership development activist, frequently speaking and consulting on *The Decision Switch*, a transformative methodology that serves to educate organizations and their leaders on the fundamental process required to make confident and productive decisions. As a result, decision-making and consistently achieving positive outcomes become core competencies and market differentiators for individuals and organizations.

Today, Jack lives in Southern California with his wife, Shannon and their daughters Makenna and Sienna. An avid sports enthusiast and adventurer seeker, if he's not cheering on his daughter's sports teams, you are likely to find him skiing, cycling, or exploring new cultures across the globe.

To connect with JACK about your speaking, consulting, or coaching needs:

Website: www.thedecisionswitch.com
Email: jack@thedecisionswitch.com

To follow JACK on social media:

- TheDecisionSwitch
- DecisionSwitch
- https://www.linkedin.com/in/jackpflaherty/
- allaboutoutput